A
Homeless
Panic

A Homeless Panic

The Homeless Experience in America

JAMES LOUGH

Edited by Randall Shaw

A HOMELESS PANIC
THE HOMELESS EXPERIENCE IN AMERICA

iUniverse books may be ordered through booksellers or by contacting:

iUniverse
1663 Liberty Drive
Bloomington, IN 47403
www.iuniverse.com
1-800-Authors (1-800-288-4677)

ISBN: 978-1-4917-8297-2 (sc)
ISBN: 978-1-4917-8298-9 (e)

Library of Congress Control Number: 2015918625

Print information available on the last page.

iUniverse rev. date: 01/07/2016

CONTENTS

FOREWORD

This book seeks to open the eyes of the fortunate to the plight of the less fortunate. It is very personal but also presents a broader look at what it means to be homeless in the United States. More than just one man's painful experience with homelessness, it provides a gripping picture of individuals living on the street and of their daily struggle to survive, doing the best they can in a desperate situation. The result is an unvarnished look at the culture of homelessness.

The gap is broad between mainstream society and the indigent. Too often, programs designed to assist homeless people serve only to alienate them. With millions of adults, teens, and children on the streets, it's time we get an idea of what people encounter when they hit the streets.

The author provides a powerful look at what it means today to be living on the street.

Randall Shaw
Editor and business executive who has been homeless

DISCLAIMER

This book is a work of nonfiction. Unless otherwise noted, the author and the publisher make no guarantees as to the accuracy of the information contained in this book. In some cases, names of people and places have been altered to protect their privacy.

ACKNOWLEDGMENTS

I would like to offer my special thanks to Randall Shaw, who did a masterful job helping me tell this story and editing it.

I wound also like to thank all the people and organizations that are involved in helping the homeless and raising awareness about this important issue.

Also my thanks go to Primosphoto.com for all the photo art in the book, and to Timeless Moments Photography for the picture of the author on the cover.

INTRODUCTION

The true story that you are about to experience takes you inside the mind of one man as he painfully encounters a world unlike any he's ever been in before. This book is about a person thrown into utter chaos when he suddenly was without a place to live. Before this turn of events, he was oblivious to the homeless crisis. But he was about to be in the fight of his life.

This story paints a vivid picture of how one person struggled to deal with the psychological pain that homelessness threw at him. Not all homeless people are able to deal with the stigma and negativity that society puts on them.

This narrative describes a world with an immense amount of misery and discontent. The impact on the main character was so great that it changed his life forever.

So open your hearts and minds to a realization that can empower you to a greater appreciation of the good things in your own life.

1

THE BEGINNING

My hands gripped the steering wheel tightly, and I wasn't focusing on the road.

Oh my God, what's happening to me?

I had no idea what I was going to do. It was like I was having an out-of-body experience of the worst kind. I'd never felt that way before. I knew I'd better pull over before I ran off the road. I needed a cup of coffee badly, but I was running very low on cash. There was a coffee shop up ahead, so I drove into the parking lot and parked in the most remote part.

I couldn't get out of the car. I'd never had an anxiety attack, but knew I was having one. My legs were shaking underneath the steering wheel. I reached across the console, grabbed my cell phone, and sat there looking at my list of contacts, then looking up at the rear-view mirror. I was actually trembling. I couldn't believe it.

Oh God, oh God! What am I gonna do? What am I gonna do?!

I had to get out of the car. People were going to start looking and wondering what I was sitting there for. When you pull into a parking lot, you're expected to get out of the car and take care of your business, whatever that is—not just sit there.

But I couldn't. I just sat there, my head filling with horrible thoughts, scaring myself.

As I walked across the parking lot, a barrage of ill feelings attacked me, reminding me of my very vulnerable situation. Yeah, it was entirely my own fault. I had made no attempt previously to develop a safety net to cushion the blow in the event that I would ever be without a place to live.

I went into the coffee shop, ordered my drink, and left.

Back in my car, I turned the ignition key to see how much gas I had in the tank. *Oh, damn, less than half a tank.* I sat back in my seat, rolling my head on the headrest, back and forth, back and forth. Then, looking up at the light pole in the parking lot, I noticed the lights had just come on.

It suddenly dawned on me that nighttime would soon be here. And for the first time in my life, there wasn't a home for me to go to. For someone who was fifty-three years old and had never worried about having a roof over his head—well, this was a dramatic change in circumstances, to say the least.

Where in the hell was I going to go? Everybody else was going home, but I couldn't.

Is this the point in my life when I fall through the cracks?

I never imagined that nighttime could be such a serious foe.

Where am I going to go? Where am I going to go? was screaming over and over in my head. Everybody was going home, but I couldn't. I didn't have a home to go to.

Still sitting there in the parking lot, I let myself get angry, cursing at people as if it were their fault. *Why doesn't someone come and rescue me? Look at those bastards. Why won't they come and save me?* (Now I see why some people lash out at society and end up on the five-o'clock news.)

But this wasn't me. I knew better. The finger pointed at me. I was just a victim of some bad decision making coupled with some rotten luck. And let's not forget arrogance. I wondered how many opportunities had passed me by, just because I wanted to be a stubborn bastard. Arrogance, that's a character trait I could have done without.

I finally started my car and slowly pulled out of the parking lot, deciding to go east on Route 9, heading toward Boston, not sure where I was going. But one thing was certain: I would be sleeping in my car tonight, wherever I ended up.

Desperation is not a state anyone chooses to be in, but I was desperate—and that's the truth.

I knew someone in the town of Natick—my friend Ed—and I thought he may be able to put me up for a while. Ed and I had known each other for ten years or so. He also knew about the death of my best friend, which was the reason I ended up on the streets. I had done some work for Ed through the years: odd jobs, painting, yard work, and things like that. Instead of calling him I decided to just knock on his door.

As I pulled into his driveway, I noticed the lights were on. I was relieved to see this sign that he was probably home. Walking up to the door, I felt embarrassed to be in my predicament. But I was gonna come right out and say I needed a place to stay for a night.

I knocked on the door and stood back, clenching my fists. I could hear someone coming to the door. It opened, and there was Ed, who appeared to be in good spirits. He opened the screen door and said, "Hello, Jim, what's going on?"

I got right to the point. "Can I park here for the night to sleep in my car?"

He seemed very receptive to me. "Sure, Jim," he said. "You can use one of the parking spaces down the hill. I'm busy with some friends of mine right now. I'll talk to you in the morning."

I owned a Volvo four-door sedan with bucket seats, so I had to sleep in the back seat if I was to have any kind of a comfortable sleep at all. Lucky for me, it was summertime, so I didn't have to deal with cold weather.

Soon it was dawn in the town of Natick, and I was waking up in the back seat of my car, without a cent and very hungry. Thirsty as hell, I rolled a window down. I heard my name being called. It was Ed, standing on top of the hill, calling me to come up. Feeling hot and sweaty, I waved at him and started up the hill.

He looked like he had a large canvas tarp in his hand. As I got close, I said, "I'm sorry for bothering you last night."

He replied, "That's okay, Jim. Take this tent, and set it up over there."

I didn't know what to think. It was a very nice Coleman four-man tent. Ed was in a very good mood, and he welcomed me to stay there on his property and camp out for a week or two. He also offered me some bottled water and a bowl of oatmeal that he had just made.

I decided that I wasn't going to drive myself crazy. I'd just calm down and take the time to plan what my next step would be.

Ed and his wife Susan invited me into their home. "Make yourself at home, Jim," he said.

"Can I make some coffee?" I asked.

"Yeah, go ahead. It's on the counter. Susan and I are stepping out. We'll be back later."

I thanked them and waved as they left. Then I found the jar of instant coffee; I just needed to heat up some water. While turning on the burner, I heard what sounded like someone coming down the stairs. The house was so big; there were rooms everywhere. A back door opened into the kitchen.

"Hello!" I said.

In walked a man who was kind of shabby, half asleep, rubbing his eyes. "Hi," he said. "Who are you?"

"Jim," I replied, "a friend of your brother."

"Oh, my name's John. How you doing?"

"I was just fixing some coffee. Would you like some?"

"Sounds good. I could use a cup."

"You are Ed's brother, right?" I asked.

"Good guess," he said. "Are you the one who's camping in the backyard?"

"Yeah, your brother is helping me out. I'm sort of without a place to stay at the moment. Temporarily homeless, if you will."

"Oh, that sucks!" he remarked. "Myself, I'm just down from Maine, visiting my family."

"I'm going to step outside and have a cigarette," I said.

"Okay, talk to you later."

While having a cigarette, I thought about the word *temporarily*. It had made me feel good to say that word as much as I could, over and over. I hoped it would be just that—temporary—and I'd soon have a place to live.

After having my coffee, I went over to the place where Ed had told me I could pitch the tent. I found a flat spot, easily set up the tent, then walked down to my car and grabbed a comforter and a couple of pillows and brought them back to the tent. Ed's brother came outside and yelled over to me, "Would you like to have a welcome mat to put down in front of your tent?"

We both laughed. He gave me the mat, and I placed it right in front. "Just like home!" I said with a big smile.

I realized that no matter what problems life dealt me, I could never abandon my sense of humor. I figured it was all that "character building" everybody talked about.

John came over and asked, "Do you want to plant some potatoes in the garden?"

"Sure, why not? I don't have anything else to do," I said.

He went on to say, "I'm a farmer in Maine, and my primary crop is fiddleheads." (Fiddlehead ferns are a traditional dish of northern New England, and especially Maine.)

"Cool. I guess that's the only way you know you're eating real food these days," I remarked.

John went over to his van and grabbed a burlap bag full of what I called baby potatoes. He corrected me, saying, "They're planting potatoes. In the garage is a shovel. Go get it, and follow me. You're going to dig the hole while I throw in the potatoes, then you fill the hole back up with dirt."

"Sounds like a plan."

After planting about six rows of potatoes, John declared, "That's enough potato planting. Thank you. Would you like something to drink?"

It was hot, and I was very thirsty. "Yes, some ice water would be good."

"I have someone I need to see. I've got to go," John said. Then he reached out to shake my hand and wished me luck.

"Nice meeting you," I said.

He jumped into his van, and he was off.

I sat down on one of the lawn chairs outside, drinking my ice water and reminding myself that I needed to figure out what to do. I already knew that a rural setting wasn't the best place to lift myself out of my homeless situation. An urban environment made more sense to me; access to more jobs, people, and places would give me many more options.

Ed and Susan came back. As Ed was getting out of the car, he asked if I was hungry and said Susan would be making dinner soon. "Sure, that would be great!" I said.

Susan was a fine cook, and it didn't take her long to whip up some dinner. After supper, I asked Ed and Susan if they wanted me to help clean up. Ed just shook his head. "No thanks, Jim."

That was music to my ears. I hadn't slept well the night before in the car, and I was looking forward to stretching out in the tent.

***

Here it is my third week of being homeless. Ed has been extremely kind to me and has welcomed me into his home. I felt he was sincere in helping me. But I still feel very vulnerable and unstable. Plus, depending on others for my own welfare isn't an acceptable situation for me.

On my last night there, I wanted to get a good night's sleep. As I stretched out in the tent, getting comfortable, I heard someone outside the tent. It was Ed. He asked what I was going to do, where I would go.

"I don't really know," I replied.

Ed suggested that I go to New York City, and then he babbled on about when he was in New York a long time ago and saw people sleeping in their cars. "They found safe places to park and sleep," he added.

I looked at Ed and said, "I'm not interested in going to New York City to sleep in my car. Massachusetts is where I'm going to stay." I thanked him for everything he had done for me and told him I needed to get some sleep.

On the following day, after a decent sleep, it was time to move on. Ed gave me a few dollars for helping him do odd jobs around the house. I thanked him again and told him I was on my way to the library to check out the Internet. He yelled out to me as I walked to my car, "Keep in touch, Jim. Let me know how you make out." I turned and waved.

The Summer Olympics were taking place in London. The election between Mitt Romney and Barack Obama was intensifying. And here I was scrambling for a place to live.

***

On the way to the library, I pulled into a gas station and got some gas. I really needed to watch my money. I didn't have much, and I didn't have a clue when I'd get more.

The library was in the city of Newton, just outside Boston, and it was huge. I'd been there before, so I knew there were plenty of computers. I sat down and got started.

I looked across the table and recognized someone I met when I'd first come to Newton. His name was Jack. We said hello to each other, and Jack asked me how things were going.

"Well," I said, "I'm no longer living in Newton. The truth is, I'm temporarily homeless."

Jack told me he was shocked. He knew I had lived in a nice home in Newton and assumed that I was doing fine. "If you don't mind me asking, what in the hell happened?"

Here is how it happened: A very good friend of mine lived with his elderly mother in a house in Newton. I became his roommate and helped take care of his mother, who had battled most of her life with severe depression. Grateful for my help, they allowed me to stay in their home.

My friend was a type 1 diabetic and needed to take insulin. However, he hated needles, which is obviously not good for a diabetic. He also ate whatever he wanted and didn't pay attention to his blood sugar levels.

After their mother passed away, my friend and his brother sold the family home that they had lived in for more than forty years. My friend moved to a single-family home in Shrewsbury. I was hesitant to relocate, but with his failing health and me being in the middle of a music project recording a five-song rock demo, it was in my best interest to make the move with him.

His condition got worse and worse. But whenever anyone told him he should go to a hospital to be checked, he got furious. Consequently, his diabetes ultimately killed him. With his passing, I no longer had a place to stay. I had lived with my friend for over ten years.

***

I got on the Internet and simply typed *homeless*. Scrolling down, I found some homeless shelters. It was all so new to me, and bad feelings were starting to creep in. I had never thought I would need to inquire about a homeless shelter. This was a sudden change, and I was not taking it well.

And no wonder. There I was in midlife, never once having given any attention to the homeless problem, indifferent to the whole enigma of homelessness. For a long time I had been secure in knowing that I had a place to lay my head at night, whether living at home, having an apartment, or just renting a room. I'd always enjoyed the comforts of some kind of *home.*

***

Consider yourself very fortunate if you can go an entire lifetime and never have to experience the feeling of being homeless. The feeling, which I wish I would have been spared, was horrible. When everything you used to enjoy, including the comfort of having your own privacy, is suddenly taken away, you are left with only two options: to live on the streets or to seek refuge in a homeless shelter.

***

One of the places on the shelter list was for the Brewster Lodge. There wasn't much on the website about it—just that it was a homeless shelter for men, where it was located, and a contact number. After writing the number down, I continued to look on the Internet to see what else was out there.

Pine Street Shelter—*no way!* I'd heard some unsavory stories about that place. Every drug addict in Boston without a place to go ended up there. Things were bad for me, I knew, but there was a limit to what I would subject myself to.

It was still early in the day, but I thought I'd better call the Brewster Lodge. I was living on the streets, and I had to find a place to stay. *I can't believe this is happening to me,* I keep repeating to myself, over and over. *A homeless person on the streets. No security! None! You're out in the cold.*

I needed to pull myself together. I got back to my car, grabbed my cell phone, and called the Brewster Lodge. A little unsure what to expect, I waited as the phone rang. Finally someone answered. "Hello, Brewster Lodge."

"Yeah, I'm calling because I'm homeless, and I am in need of a place to stay," I muttered, embarrassed.

The woman asked if she could ask me a series of questions. "That's okay," I said, also mentioning to her that I had been homeless for about three weeks. She seemed understanding and pleasant. After I answered the questions, she began to tell me a little about the shelter, informing me that the Brewster was a "dry" shelter. I didn't have a clue what a dry shelter was, but she went on to explain that a dry shelter doesn't allow anyone who drinks or is a drug user. And all residents were subject to random drug testing.

She also told me that I needed to show up for what they call an "intake"—the shelter's screening procedure for new residents—between four and six.

"Okay," I said and thanked her. We were done until my intake.

Sitting in my car, looking at my map to see where the shelter was, I was thinking about some of the questions the woman had asked me. I had been very uncomfortable being subjected to them: Are you homicidal? Are you suicidal? Have you ever abused an elderly person? I mean, come on, does falling into homelessness automatically put you in the same category with murderers and lunatics? Well, the people at the Brewster Lodge apparently thought so.

I was angry but needed a place to stay. Having a bed to sleep in that night was more important to me than defending my good name. I ended up telling myself that they probably had a good reason for asking the kind of questions they did, but it didn't make you feel any better about it. The uncertainty of everything made me feel uneasy. I no longer had the familiarity and the privilege of having my own place.

The sudden shock of losing everything was also disturbing my usual thought process. And I was feeling growing resentment that I was living that way. A Dunkin' Donuts restroom was my bathroom. Suddenly, it was clear to me that I was living on the streets.

I had a couple of hours to kill before my intake at the Brewster. I should have been depressed as hell, but I wasn't. Homelessness can bring harsh feelings, but my personality didn't allow me to stop and dwell on them too long. I considered that a plus.

Everything that we do is centered on the home, and I knew that was what I was going to reclaim. A home is the foundation of our existence, whether it's an apartment, a room, or living in the basement of your mother's house. Any dwelling is better than no dwelling. Shelter is our security. Without it, I had a cold, empty feeling that I wouldn't wish on anyone. Everything looks dismal from the street.

Feeling anxious before my appointment at the Brewster Lodge, I didn't want to drive around and waste gas, so I sat in the car, listening to my radio. A very good song was playing, but I wasn't into it. There was nothing on the radio that interested me. I was consumed by my homeless situation, and things I used to enjoy just weren't the same. Music, television, movies— how easily they lost their thrill. The amount of enjoyment they used to give me just wasn't the same once I was homeless.

I knew for certain that I could not let myself fall down any further. When bad things happen to people, there can be a domino effect. People can give up, stop caring, and end up turning to alcohol and drugs. And it spirals out of control from there.

***

It was getting close to four o'clock, time to be heading to the shelter for my intake. Driving up Elm Street, I spotted the address. There was a parking lot right across the street. I pulled in and parked my car. Walking across the street, I could see what looked like a fire station. I yelled to someone walking by, asking if he had ever heard of the Brewster Lodge. He pointed toward a set of stairs on the side of the fire station.

Walking up the stairs, I saw a sign that read, "Please ring the buzzer." I pushed the button, waited, pushed again, waited, and pushed again. Someone finally buzzed me in. As I climbed more stairs, I was very aware of my surroundings. The place seemed reasonably clean. Why that was important to me, I don't know. It just was.

Beyond another door were a few more stairs to climb. As I stood in a small hallway, someone walked over and asked me if my name was James. I told him yes. "My name is Robbie," he said. We shook hands, and he told me to come with him.

Robbie took me to a small office at the end of the hall and asked me to have a seat. Then he asked me for some identification. I showed him my driver's license and Social Security card. He then explained a little about the Brewster Lodge and told me he had some forms for me to fill out.

But first he had a string of questions he needed to ask me, things like if I'd recently been to a foreign country, if I had any illnesses, HIV, or AIDS. I responded no to all his questions. He also wanted to know my age, where I was born, things like that. Then I filled out and signed a couple of forms.

Robbie told me he was *not* going to give me a urine test. That was fine with me! He also mentioned that I had to get a TB (tuberculosis) test within two weeks. "If you don't get a TB certificate stating that your test is negative, you will be kicked out," he added.

Robbie told me the shelter's policies while giving me a tour of the facility, showing me each room. There were two dorm rooms where the guests slept in bunk beds. One held eight, and the larger room held up to forty. He assigned me a number that corresponded to my bed, which was in the small dorm room. That sounded good to me. Another room Robbie showed me was where the guests could watch TV. He also mentioned that the TV went off at eleven o'clock.

Then he showed me the kitchen, which also held two washing machines and two dryers. Each guest was assigned a locker as well. The lockers were at three levels, one on top of the other, cramped along two walls in the kitchen.

I didn't like the bathroom situation at all. There were no doors and no stalls, so the toilets were open, with no privacy at all. That was absolutely awful. It was so bad that some of the guests would take a piss in the shelter, but nothing else. But, of course, having a place to sleep at night was the most important thing; I could live with the open toilets.

Robbie then told me that we had to be out of the shelter by 7:45 a.m., seven days a week. And the arrival policy was equally as strict: everyone had to be in the shelter by seven in the evening. They could arrive at four but no earlier.

Robbie also asked me if I smoked. I said yes. He said that the first smoke break was at 5:30 p.m., then at seven and then every hour until eleven. Smoke breaks were fifteen minutes long. Anyone caught smoking other than the designated times would be restricted (kicked out) for one week.

Guests were allowed to stay at the shelter for ninety days. After that, they had to leave for thirty days before they could come back. And thirty days meant thirty days (not four weeks).

Robbie asked me if I had any questions. I told him no. I was tired and just wanted to get some sleep. He went to his office to get me linens for my bed.

Well, that was it. I was in, a guest at the Brewster Lodge. Making my bed and getting some sleep was the only thing on my mind. When you become homeless you're always tired, because your normal sleep regimen is disrupted terribly.

Looking around, I noticed that they were using bunk beds, which were absolutely horrible. The mattresses were thin, and the pillows were more like doormats than pillows. If I hadn't told myself that it was better than living on the streets, somebody around there would remind me.

My first night's sleep at the Brewster was solid. I had forgotten what a good sleep felt like. For me, taking a shower and changing into some clean clothes was first on my agenda. The guests told me the showers ran out of hot water fast, so we often had to take cold showers.

You would think a shelter that accommodated only forty-eight people wouldn't feel crowded. But it did, mainly due to the small amount of space. From what I could see, the shelter would be better suited for housing twenty guests. It sure would have been a lot less congested.

Looking for a job was my main objective. I decided I'd spend my day at the library using their computers to surf the Internet for some work. Hopefully something would come up.

Matt, one of the guests, and I were talking and kind of introducing ourselves. This was his second time at the shelter. I asked him, "Was the coffee here as bad the first time you were here?"

He replied, "At least it's free."

"That doesn't make it taste any better."

Matt knew some of the people at the shelter. He told me who was cool and who was not so cool, but I was going to make up my own mind. We were making small talk as we went out the door and down the stairs. Everyone went their separate ways.

I walked across the street to check out my car. I liked having a place to park it so close to the shelter. It sure made things easier.

I sat in the car, listening to some original rock music that some musician friends and I had recorded before my world was turned upside down. I grabbed my cell phone and started calling anyone who might be able to lend me some money. I didn't have a rich uncle to ask for money. And my brother and sisters were all grown up with families of their own, and money was tight.

But a musician friend I knew from high school, Dan, was able to send me fifty bucks via MoneyGram. That was so cool of him. We went way back and had a lot of good times back then. He obviously didn't forget.

I didn't have much success finding work on the Internet, so I went outside the library to have a cigarette. I ended up talking to someone who was also staying at the Brewster. He told me about a church that served dinner at five every day. He also mentioned that the food was pretty good.

Being on the street, you inevitably meet new people every day. So many have fallen on hard times. I wasn't too worried about being out on the streets; having grown up in a city certainly helped me get by a little easier as a homeless person. Waltham isn't Baltimore (the city I grew up in), but it's still loud with a lot of people, and it moves relatively fast.

I knew getting better oriented with my surroundings would help me feel more at ease. I hadn't been able to venture out too far from Waltham. Money was very short, and I needed to ration what little gas I had in the car. Trying to conserve on cigarettes was going to be hard. If people knew you smoked, they'd hound you for one all the time.

"The soup kitchen is open," someone said to me as he walked by. "Dinner is at five, but they have coffee and snacks starting around three."

"Sounds good. I'll be there," I replied.

I went back to my car to check out the phone numbers of some people I knew to see if I could drum up some work—odd jobs, anything. I really needed to make some money. Looking up, I noticed Matt walking toward my car. "Hey, what are you doing?" he asked.

"Getting ready to head up to the soup kitchen and grab some coffee."

Matt knew the soup kitchen and had eaten there before. "Can I hitch a ride with you?" he asked.

"Let's go," I said.

***

For the first time in my life I was at the mercy of a soup kitchen, standing in line for a free meal. Oddly, the shame in coming to a place like that went away—especially after meeting some of the people who ran the kitchen. They were really fine folks. The food was plentiful and good.

And engaging in conversation and the chance to meet new people was a plus. I saw a lot of people who were staying at the Brewster as well.

Someone sitting across from me told me that it was more crowded at the end of the month than the beginning of the month because people typically get money—like paychecks, food stamps, and disability checks—earlier in the month. They eat out, and sadly some squander their checks on alcohol and don't bother going to the soup kitchen. Not that they would be welcome there anyway; the kitchen had a no-drinking policy. The kitchen staff did their best to maintain order.

Many times in the past I'd heard the term "soup kitchen." It was something I always looked down on or was completely indifferent toward. But the tables had turned, so along with my dinner, I had a large helping of humble pie.

Strolling up Moody Street to the soup kitchen.

High-end condo for the wealthy, a stark contrast to the
homeless on the way to the soup kitchen.

2

THE SHELTER

I had been a guest for two full weeks at the Brewster Lodge, a homeless shelter. And I was thinking, *Give me a break! Is this the best they can do?* I mean, it was a slap in the face to any good, decent human being. Those bastards with their degrees in sociology or positions in the Department of Human Services. I mean, people who most likely had never experienced homelessness themselves were trying to plot a way back for those who had fallen victim to a terrible situation.

And they held the cards. It was their way or the highway. If you couldn't take it or didn't like standing in the rain, you had to take what they offered and suck it up.

The Brewster was on the top floor in an old, deserted fire station. It had those two dorm rooms, a small kitchen, two bathrooms, and a small TV room. There were three offices for administrative and management personnel that all connect to a very cramped hallway. The kitchen was even smaller due to the fact that the lockers for each guest and laundry facilities were all crowded in the same room. There was one refrigerator, no stove, and one small microwave (that even worked sometimes)—for forty-eight people.

If you were to ask anyone at the shelter about the conditions there, they would tell you that the Brewster Lodge was one of the best homeless shelters in the state. But these same people did nothing but complain about the cramped living quarters, unreasonable shelter policies, and on and on. It was really sad.

I wasn't looking for a stay at the Hilton Hotel nor was I ungrateful for what the shelter provided. I understood that the problem of homelessness was at least being addressed; some effort was being made to help homeless people in Massachusetts. And that was why Massachusetts could be the ideal state to push for improving conditions for the homeless. It could be a model, if you will, for other states to follow.

There was one commonality that applied to everyone there: *nobody really wanted to be there.* I mean, not just there at the shelter, but there as in being homeless. But, of course, the degree of urgency to change things and get back to having a normal life differs from person to person. Some give up. Others want to change their lives, but don't know how. And there are those who *can't stand* being homeless and work very hard to change their situation.

***

Someone was yelling, "Smoke break!" throughout the shelter. It was a good time for conversation, meeting new people, talking about what you did during the day, etc.

Time to go to bed. I was up early every morning, and the next day I had a date with a temporary job agency. From what I'd been hearing, the pay wasn't that great, but anything was better than zero.

It was a bad time to be homeless. Our economy was having a meltdown, and jobs were hard to come by. Most people at the shelter went to the library in town to use computers for job hunting, but that didn't pay the bills, especially when you came up empty at the end of the day.

It's funny how dealing with life's obstacles can reflect a truer image of you than any mirror can.

If someone would have come up to me, even just one month before I became homeless, and asked me if I would ever find myself out on the streets with no place to live, my answer would have been an emphatic no.

***

I got a job at Labor Force, and the orientation was easy enough. But the pay was lousy. Yet everyone who worked for them would say, "It's better than nothing." I'd just nod my head and reply, "Yeah, yeah, you know it." Looking around, I could see that those folks had fallen on hard times as well. Why else would they be there?

During my first month at the Brewster, my living standards hit an all-time low. I guess there's something to be said about how your environment can affect your attitude. I mean, here I was, surrounded by homeless people, and now I was working for an agency that exploited people by sending them to perform jobs that most people in their right minds wouldn't do. Being around all that negativity wasn't good.

One day, walking back to the shelter, I saw Matt. "What are you doing?" I asked.

"Oh, just looking for a winner," he replied. Matt was rummaging through trash cans, examining already used scratch tickets (the state lottery) to see if anyone had thrown away a winning ticket. There were a few people I'd seen around town doing that, picking them up off the ground, even going into convenience stores to inspect trash cans where people discarded losing scratch tickets. And just to lend credit to those who partake in that venture, sometimes they did find a winning ticket.

***

Another rise-and-shine morning at the Brewster, but it wasn't starting out so good. There seemed to be a shouting match going on out in the hallway. Someone was yelling at a guy for turning off the fan during the night in the big dorm room. Tensions often ran very high around there.

I climbed down from my top bunk, washed up, got dressed, had a quick cup of coffee, and was out the door. The earlier a person showed up at Labor Force, the better the job assignments he got.

I was the second one through the door. Mickey, the manager at Labor Force said good morning.

"Good morning," I replied and signed in.

"Hey, Jim, do you want to go to Burlington? It's a nine-hour day."

"Sure," I responded. "I can use the hours."

Mickey explained the job to me. I would be moving furniture around, picking up debris, things like that. "Okay, let's do it!" I said.

Having a car made it easier for me to get a good assignment. But, of course, I had to take along other people. We carpooled because most people at the shelter and at Labor Force didn't have a car. So we piled in and took off.

I made a quick stop at the gas station, and then we were on our way. (Labor Force gave people who had a car some incentive by making anyone who rode with them pay five dollars for gas.)

Looking in my rear-view mirror, I asked Steve how he was doing. "Okay," Steve replied. He was from Africa and didn't speak English too well, but he was a great worker.

Our day was long and hard, but we got through it. It was typical Labor Force grunt work. But it was time to head back and get paid.

Matt wanted to know what I was doing for supper. "Let's go to the market," I said, "and pick up some bison and cook it back at the shelter."

"Sure! Sounds good! Bison burgers, yum!" Bison was cheaper than ground beef, as well as being better for you.

Once back at the shelter, Matt prepared to start cooking the burgers. Everybody knew that if you wanted to make supper at the shelter, you'd better be the first one there, or you'd be waiting around for the few available kitchen utensils. The burgers were excellent.

After a smoke break, I headed up to my dorm room, because I needed to fill out a job application. But before I could climb up to my bed, there was a disturbance outside my dorm room. Two men had started shouting at each other, and things started to get ugly. It sounded like all hell was breaking loose, and two of the guests were fighting. They were pushing and shoving and yelling at each other.

The staff tried to intervene, but it escalated, and ultimately the police had to be called in to break it up. So much for a peaceful night at the shelter. You stick forty-eight men in cramped and stressful living quarters, and there will inevitably be discord.

Once things settled down, I finally got some sleep.

I woke up a little earlier than usual. *That's okay,* I told myself. *I'll do my laundry and take a shower.*

The kitchen light was on, and there was Art, making coffee. Art had spent a lot of time there at the shelter—actually many years. We called him King Arthur. He was probably the most recognizable homeless person in Waltham.

"Hey, Art," I said.

"Morning, Jim. Do you want some coffee?"

"Sure!" I replied.

I didn't hear the washing machines going, so I decided to do my laundry. Finding an open washing machine was difficult; there was always a long wait. I looked around the corner to see if anybody was in the office. Jason, one of two staff persons on duty then, was there, watching TV.

I wanted to sneak out the back door off the kitchen to have a smoke. Smoking cigarettes before six thirty wasn't permitted, so I was taking a risk. If I was caught smoking before then, they could kick me out of the shelter for up to two weeks. Art was cool; I knew he wouldn't rat me out. It was just a typical early morning at the Brewster.

After my shower, I thought I'd throw my clothes in the dryer. "Hey," I said to Jason. "I need a towel."

"I need some ID," Jason replied.

"Oh yeah," I said. That was another policy at the shelter. Because some guests didn't always return their towels, the shelter started making everyone leave their ID at the office whenever they borrowed one. Imagine! We had to leave our driver's license to get a towel. Oh well, gotta do what you gotta do. Typically the shelter would require IDs for towels for a couple of weeks and then stop—until the next time a towel didn't return.

The shower was great, plenty of hot water. While waiting for my clothes to dry, I thought I'd make my bed. That was another rule: your bed had to be made before you left for the day—or you could be restricted.

The only place you could talk in the morning was in the kitchen, so you didn't disturb those still sleeping. But there were always people who had no consideration for others and talked anywhere they wanted.

I hoped that someday I'd wake up and this would have been just a nightmare.

My laundry was dry. After putting on some fresh clothes, I needed to get going. I went out the door and down the stairs, and as I walked to my car, I ran into Matt, who was also heading to Labor Force. "Hey, do you want a ride?" I asked.

"Yeah," Matt replied.

When we got to the car, I noticed something leaking from the engine.

"Oh shit!" Matt said. "It looks like tranny fluid!"

Oh boy, that was all I needed, for my car to break down. I told Matt, "Get in. I'll check my transmission fluid later."

"Why don't we check out your car at Labor Force?" Matt suggested.

Pulling into the parking lot, I noticed what I thought was smoke coming from the hood of my car. Matt suggested I pull up to the sidewalk and pop the hood.

He got out of the car and raised the hood. Still sitting in the car, I yelled, "What's wrong? What's up?"

Matt gave me a thumbs-down. I jumped out of the car to see for myself. The radiator was leaking fluid all over the place. "It's your radiator, Jim," Matt said. The top of my radiator was cracked. And I knew it was going to be an expensive repair job.

My car was out of commission until I could come up with money to fix it. I knew someone who could repair it, but how long it was going to take me to come up with the cash was anybody's guess.

Matt was standing there, rolling one of his roll-your-own cigarettes. "That sucks," he muttered. "You're talking six, seven hundred dollars to replace the radiator."

"Oh man! What am I going to do? I can't leave it here."

"What's wrong, Jim?" I turned around to see who was asking. It was Alex, an older Russian fellow who also worked at Labor Force. I responded, "My radiator is shot!"

Then, in his heavy Russian accent, he asked me, "What are you going to do?"

I just shook my head. "I don't know. I can't leave it here. I have to find somewhere to park it until I can come up with the money to have it repaired."

"How long will it be before you can have it fixed?" Alex asked.

"I don't know, maybe a month or so."

"You can keep it at my house," he offered.

I turned and looked at Matt. "Hey, Matt, let's walk over to the auto supply store so I can pick up some radiator fluid." It was just across the street.

As we walked, Matt said it was so good of Alex to let me keep my car over at his house. "You know it!" I said. "But it's going to take a long time for me to save that much money. Just working at Labor Force, it isn't going to be easy coming up with the money I need."

Then I added with some hesitation, "Well, I'm on foot now."

Matt smiled and jokingly said, "It isn't that bad. You'll have to get a bus card now."

"Oh fun!" I replied.

It had been a long time since I'd had to depend on public transportation. Oh well! I had no choice. I'd just have to make the best of it. "I'll see you back at the shelter," I said to Matt. I went back to my car and put some antifreeze in the radiator. "Lead on, Alex," I said. "I'll follow."

Because I was working at Labor Force, it would take me forever to accumulate a thousand dollars for the repair. After everyday expenses, there wasn't much left for putting away savings for car repair.

It felt weird showing up at Labor Force without my car. I was on the other side of the fence, meaning I was one of those who needed a ride to the job site instead of giving one. That also meant I had to shell out five bucks to whoever I rode with. And when I coupled that with the lousy pay, it was almost counterproductive to even show up.

I had to find something better.

***

Walking up the steps to go into the shelter, I noticed someone sitting on the stairs. It looked like he was loaded down with a lot of baggage: a backpack, duffle bag, and other stuff. Robbie opened the door but told the guy that he couldn't come into the Brewster because he was drunk. I felt sorry for him. It was cold and rainy, and he apparently had no other place to go.

Robbie was always helping people out, but that time he just couldn't. There were limits to what he could do; if he ignored those limits, his own job was in jeopardy.

Walking by the office, I yelled out my bed number. That's what we did to let them know we were in for the night. I didn't feel like fraternizing with the other guests. Sleeping was the only thing on my mind. Five o'clock in the morning came quickly.

Life in the shelter was having a big effect on me. I had to make a lot of adjustments to survive. Instead of sleeping in my own bed in my own room, I was sharing a room with seven other people. No one wanted to complain out loud; it was just something we dealt with.

It was my first experience in a shelter, and I didn't know who to trust. One night, one of my friends at the shelter told me about an experience that shocked him. He was an accountant and always knew exactly how much money he had on him at all times. However, he had misplaced a five-dollar bill and, of course, expected that he would never see that money again.

But he was surprised when the guy in the bunk above him asked if he was missing anything. My friend replied that he'd lost five dollars. That's when the bunk mate handed him a five-dollar bill that he'd found lying on their dorm-room floor that morning. So, even in a homeless shelter, there are honest people who undoubtedly had a solid upbringing.

To avoid the morning rush hour at the shelter, waking up early seemed to be a working strategy for me. I had my coffee, got dressed, and headed out the door.

Labor Force had given me a decent work assignment: a job that would keep me working full time for up to four weeks. It didn't start till eight, so I had time to have another coffee at the corner store, play a couple of scratch tickets, and shoot the bull with a few friends I'd met at Labor Force.

My goof-ball humor usually attracted knuckleheads. And soon we would have "back of the classroom" antics going on. It was good for morale. I didn't like my current situation, but making the best of a bad situation was all I had.

I found that the people I met, the ones I got acquainted with, were important to my overall well-being. That's saying a lot. No one has to suffer alone.

Having other people to interact with helped slow me down and think of others instead of just myself. However, I sometimes found myself being condescending toward everyone and everything. And that was *not good.*

I had trouble accepting my current living situation and yearned so much for a better life. Controlling what I was mindful of could be so overwhelming that it totally weirded me out. I guess what I'm saying is that I was getting too stressed out. I needed to get it together.

I didn't want to accept the homeless lifestyle at all. I was very mindful not to make the mistake of finding my comfort zone there.

I'd work any job. I'd look for work on the computer at the local library on the days I wasn't working at Labor Force. I'd do whatever I had to, in order to buy some time until something better came along. The thought of living from shelter to shelter and eating at soup kitchens for a long period scared the hell out of me.

***

One thing that was becoming more and more clear to me was that all homeless people don't think alike. They differ greatly in their sense of urgency in getting themselves free from homelessness. And for any person, group, or organization that tries to take on the homeless problem, understanding this distinction can enable them to better understand the homeless population and develop more effective ways to combat this serious problem.

Many people across the country are involved in addressing the homeless problem. I am just a "Johnny come lately" when it comes to dealing with this crisis. But becoming homeless really gave me a wake-up call to what's happening in our country. Having experienced it personally has given me a valuable perspective that I would like to share.

Where I had to spend a couple of nights when there was no other place to go.

I can only imagine that the homeless problem has been around for a long, long time. Becoming homeless has led me to try to come up with some answers regarding why people become homeless and how to fix it. I want to do my part and better understand this growing problem.

The Massachusetts Coalition for the Homeless has statistics that they put on the Internet for anyone who's interested (www.mahomeless.org). According to them, the number of homeless people in the state of Massachusetts has more than doubled since 1990, and in the month of January 2013 there were an estimated 19,129 homeless people right in my own beloved Commonwealth.

You know they don't get everyone when they do a headcount like that. It wouldn't surprise me if that number was much higher.

***

Time was going by quickly, and I needed to figure out where I was going to stay when my ninety days were up.

Back at the shelter, there was quite a congregation of guests standing around in the hallway, with many conversations going on at once. I was meeting some very cool people at the Brewster, one in particular. His name was Daniel. He was from New Bedford, Massachusetts. He had come to the Brewster to try to get away from his cronies and get off a heroin addiction. Whenever he'd go back home, he'd go right back to the junk. He claimed to be thirty-six days off heroin.

He was the kind of person you really root for: great personality and very popular at the shelter. You could tell that Daniel didn't have a pretentious bone in his body. He'd literally give you the shirt off his back.

He wanted to know what I was doing that day. I reluctantly told him I was working down at Labor Force. He laughed and said he'd worked there before and planned to go back. I rolled my eyes and muttered, "Gee, that's too bad."

"Yeah, yeah, I know they suck," he said.

"Well, I guess I'll see you down there tomorrow," I said. I was tired and needed to get to bed.

He asked me what time I was waking up. I told him five.

"Can you wake me up when you get up?" he asked. I explained to him that they did wake-up calls here at the Brewster. "Just go to the office and give them your bed number and the time you want to be up, and they'll do it. Good night!"

The following morning, I was heading to work when I saw a man pushing a shopping cart with big, green plastic bags loaded with aluminum cans. As I was passing him, I turned to him and said, "If I don't get my shit together, I'm going to be you in five years."

He had a blank expression on his face. I mean, it was like I was talking to a stone. Man! You talk about being hardened from a rough life.

I felt bad afterward. When I first spotted him, I was thinking, *Is that my future staring me right in the face?* Weird! It left me wishing I hadn't said anything at all to him.

It was six in the morning, and it looked like there were more people than usual at Labor Force. The front doors were always swinging open—people going to jobs, people waiting around to see if they were going to be lucky and get a job for the day. Meanwhile, they'd stand outside and have a cigarette, shooting the bull to anybody who'd listen.

Then came the boss to tell everyone to go stand to the side of the building, not in front. Everyone would piss and moan, but they moved. Just another day at Labor Force.

It was a hassle when you didn't have a car. You'd always try to line up a ride to get to and from the job site. At least for the short term, I didn't have to worry about that. There was only one other person assigned to the job with me, and fortunately he had a car.

The workday was longer than usual—a lot of heavy lifting and clean-up detail. After work, I wanted to sit down and figure out how much money I could save each day. But the tides were working against me. I mean, when you subtracted your daily expenses from a Labor Force paycheck, you usually ended up with one stinking buck left over. And to make matters worse, someone would walk up to you and say, "Hey, it ain't that bad. You're halfway to a pack of Double Diamonds." What a laugh! For those who don't know what Double Diamonds are, they're miniature cigars, but packaged like cigarettes. Picking up a stick off the ground and smoking it was about the same thing. I've seen even heavy smokers refuse those damn things when trying to bum a cigarette. I think that shows a little class, doesn't it? No matter how sorry and miserable your life is, you can still be a little discriminating at times.

Working a full day was cool, but it usually made you miss the five o'clock dinner over at the soup kitchen. That meant more money you had to shell out for food. Oh well, what are you going to do?

Heading to the supermarket to get some food, I'd run into people who were also staying at the shelter, coming back from the soup kitchen. I'd always ask them what they had for dinner. "Oh! You missed a good one!" they'd say. And then they'd run down the whole menu. It mostly made me pissed off because I missed it.

After making sandwiches back at the shelter, I'd find a corner in the kitchen to sit in and eat. I'd looked up to see who was coming through the door and greet the ones I recognized.

"Hey, John!"

John replied, "Jim, how are you?"

This guy was fun to be around—an Irishman straight from the fatherland. If there was ever a wanderer, John was one. And he seemed to like it. He had an adventurous spirit and always had a story to tell. John told me what he did each day.

He said one time he'd had a funny but embarrassing moment at a mall parking lot. When the police tapped on his car window, John's head suddenly appeared from under a couple of pillows. The expression on the cop's face was hilarious. There was a guy emerging from a pile of blankets and stuff. I could imagine Macy's department store as a backdrop.

When John told me his escapades out on the road, living in his car, he always had me bent over in laughter. And the way he expressed himself, punctuated with his heavy Irish accent, was very funny.

***

And that's what we do, isn't it? We humans have the uncanny ability to take an otherwise bleak circumstance, turn it around, and make a joke out of it. Yeah, when you become homeless, you're just a statistic, the butt end of a joke.

I once heard a radio talk show host ripping the homeless. He made a mockery of the whole homeless crisis. But he was using some bad examples of homeless people to represent the homeless problem as a whole. He was talking about the very opportunistic types who exploit their dilemma for financial gain, willing to be looked on with pity, hoping that some sympathetic bleeding heart will throw money at them. There are people like that. But that isn't the type of person I include when I speak of the homeless.

Most would not take something for nothing. They are quiet, dignified, hard-working people who, for one reason or another, fell by the wayside. I'd never realized this before, but homelessness can kill. And I can imagine that it's a long and miserable death.

***

My cell phone was ringing. "Hello, it's Marie from Labor Force. Jim, can you come in a little earlier tomorrow? I need some people for an early morning job." I reminded her that I already had a work assignment—full time.

"Oh yeah, you're working in Burlington, aren't you?"

"That's right," I said.

"Sorry to bother you, Jim." And she hung up.

It was eleven thirty at night, and she was calling me. What? Was she crazy? Damn! Those people were relentless—as well as inconsiderate.

It was time for me to catch some shut-eye. Sometimes it was difficult to fall asleep, especially when I got to bed later than I normally did. There was always somebody snoring loudly.

The next morning, I was standing outside Labor Force talking to Matt about finding a better job. The idea was to find an employer who used Labor Force to outsource labor and try to convince said employer to hire you to work full time directly for the company, with no middle man—in our case, no Labor Force.

Matt extended his arm and started pointing. I turned to look and saw Alex pulling into one of the parking spaces. "It must be Friday," Matt exclaimed. Labor Force sent drivers out to drive cars at auto auctions. Alex was one of their drivers. He also was the fellow who was letting me park my car in his driveway until I could get it repaired.

"Hello, Jim, how are you doing?" asked Alex.

"Hey, Alex, not bad. At least I'm working."

Then he asked me how much money I'd saved so far.

"Gee, Alex. I haven't been able to save much. Maybe a hundred."

"Jim," Alex replied in that low Russian tone of his, "I want to help you, but I don't know for how long. My wife is starting to complain about the car in the driveway."

All I could do was stand there and plead with him for more time. Holding on to my car while I came up with the money to repair it was proving to be a big pain in the neck.

***

The workday was shorter than usual. That meant I was able to make the five o'clock dinner at the soup kitchen. I was sitting at my usual spot at the soup kitchen, waiting for our table number to be called out. Someone led us in the Lord's Prayer. Giving grace was protocol at the soup kitchen before dinner began. Oh well, it was in the basement of a church, after all.

The dinner looked good: fried chicken, French fries, tossed salad, and chocolate cake. Yum! Most of the time, there was enough food for everyone to have seconds. The soup kitchen would have food brought in from corporations, such as IBM, and a number of church groups throughout eastern Massachusetts. Local restaurants in the community would also often donate food to the kitchen.

"Hey, Jim, could you spare an extra cigarette?"

"Sure, Mike. Here you go."

Mike was one of the guests over at the Brewster. There were a lot of people with the same name staying there. Among the most popular names were *Dave* and *Mike*.

He asked me if I was heading back to the shelter. I told him yes, just after I cleared my tray. I always would thank the kitchen staff as I headed out the door.

Waiting at the top of the stairs, Mike asked me if I had a light. "Gee, Mike. Do you want me to smoke it for you too?" I said.

Mike grinned as I lit his cigarette. Then he and I talked about how the meal was. The chocolate cake was so fresh I had to have two pieces.

"Get it while you can," Mike added.

One of the constants in a conversation between two people residing at the Brewster was how much time you had left before your ninety days were up. My number was ten—ten days to go. After that, I would need to find a place to stay for at least thirty days. That was the amount of time you had to be out of the shelter before returning.

There's no rest for the homeless. You're constantly worrying about where you're going to stay next.

I needed to see Robbie to get a list of all the homeless shelters in the area. Not having my car narrowed it down a little. Logistics mattered a great deal in my circumstances. It would serve me well to stay in an urban environment and take advantage of public transportation. It was the only choice I really had that made sense.

I had, on occasion, toyed around with the idea of traveling somewhere far away and making a new start. To be adventurous was a wonderful thing, but as logic would have it, staying put and working out my problems in a more familiar place was the best way to go.

***

Later that evening, back at the Brewster, someone was complaining about a mouse that had gotten into his breakfast cereal. This was a fairly routine problem around there. Sometimes if you got up early enough and went into the kitchen, you could hear the mice munching on the food. The staff may have set up traps, but in reality, the mice were guests at the shelter the same as we were. As for me, I never stored food in the shelter. I couldn't afford to feed the mice.

After watching some movies in the TV room, I decided to go to bed. Walking into the small dorm room, I just wanted to get to my bunk and sleep. But there seemed to be some trouble going on.

Tony had been tying his boots. But he put his boot on the edge of someone else's bed to do it. Lou, who was lying in his bunk, flipped out and pushed Tony's foot from his bunk bed. "Don't put your dirty shoes *on my bed!*" he shouted.

This was all I need—Lou, an ex-con, and Tony the instigator going at it. But Tony did not back down, and the next thing I knew, there was about to be a fight right there in the small dorm room.

"*Jesus!* Come on guys, take it easy," I said. To Tony, I added, "If you get into it with Lou, the Brewster will throw you out. You don't want that, do you? You just got here!"

Meanwhile, Lou was yelling at Tony, threatening to go to the office and complain.

"Do what you gotta do, man!" Tony replied, laughing and waving his hand, mocking him.

I didn't know either Lou or Tony that well. But I thought I would have a better chance to calm the situation by dealing with Tony. Lou seemed to have some serious anger issues. In the end, it seemed that my words to Tony had a positive effect in preventing a fight. Things settled down, and I was finally able to get some sleep.

Well, that was my last weekend at the Brewster. Come Monday, I had to find another shelter. When I was talking to the other guests, telling them my time was about up, one of them asked me where I was going to go. I told him I wasn't sure. The only logical choice seemed to be the Cambridge homeless shelter run by a well-known international charitable organization.

Most of the shelters on the list Robbie gave me were either wet shelters or too far out of the way. I needed to be someplace where I could access the bus so I could get to work.

It was just a short walk from the Brewster Lodge to Labor Force. From Cambridge, I would have to take two buses to get to work.

***

Of all the mandatory rules that existed at the Brewster, having to be out by seven forty-five, seven days a week, was very effective in enforcing structure and keeping those who come to the shelter "honest." It drove residents to seek an alternative means of support and a way out of the shelter. In many ways, it mimicked the hustle and bustle of everyday life.

A crucial component in helping people rectify their homeless situation is *time*. And that's what you got at the Brewster. They purposely didn't want anyone to get too comfortable there. Well, I can be the first to tell you that they didn't have any problem with guests getting too comfortable, that's for sure!

If I were running the show, I would give the residents *more* time: 120 days rather than ninety. And instead of being out for thirty days, they could make it forty days out, since there was so much demand for space in the shelter. Homelessness is a dreadful situation to be in, and I just don't think ninety days gives people enough time to get themselves back on their feet.

3

MEAN STREETS

I hopped on a bus heading to Watertown Square, where I then caught the 71 bus to Central Square in Cambridge. I was hoping to get a bed for the night at the homeless shelter of an international charitable organization—Ally's, as it was referred to on the streets. It was raining and cold out.

As I was walking up Mass Av (Massachusetts Avenue, but the locals always just said "Mass Av"), some people were coming up to me, selling drugs. I was as cold as the temperature outside, walking fast and deliberately paying no mind to those jokers, thinking, *Get the hell away from me!*

And there was the shelter. As I walked in the door, I noticed a couple of people in the foyer. One of them told me that they didn't see anybody before 7:30 p.m.

I had about a thirty-minute wait. I thought I might try calling my brother, who lived in California, for some money—again. Knowing it was going to be a wasted call, I did it anyway. "Hello, brother John," I said. "How are you doing? How's your family?"

"Hi, Jim," he responded. I could already sense his *I can't be bothered with this call* tone. I told him I wasn't doing so good and needed some money. I explained that I was standing in the rain in Cambridge, Massachusetts, waiting to sign in at a homeless shelter.

Being very conscious about my prepaid cell phone minutes, I began speaking to him like a high-powered salesman rather than a brother.

John's a philosophical kind of guy, always generalizing about the ways of the world. It was like he was purposely dancing around my question, as if he was avoiding my request and not being direct with me. He is soft-spoken, and when I heard the words "Yeah, Jim, I'll see what I can do," I knew that meant no.

It was no one's fault but my own. I did owe him some money already and had never made an attempt to pay it back. My credit was finished as far as my brother was concerned.

There was some movement going on at the entrance to the shelter. *Must be time to check in,* I thought.

As I entered the building, I heard some shouting among people I thought were running the shelter, yelling out somebody's name. A tall, thin African-American man asked me what I wanted. I told him I was homeless and I needed a place to stay for the night. He then asked me, "Is this your first time here at the shelter?" I said yes. Then he told me to stand to the side. He was going to check to see if there were any open beds.

Oh boy, that was all I needed to hear. I didn't have any other place in mind to go. Wandering the streets of Cambridge, looking for a place to lie down, was not at all appealing to me.

Nobody received a warm welcome at that shelter, that's for sure. Looking around, I wasn't impressed. I mean, this was the homeless shelter of a large international organization. Millions were donated to that organization every year. From the looks of it, none of that money made it here.

The fellow came back to me and asked me a few questions. Had I been in a homeless shelter before? Did I have an alcohol or drug use problem? I told him I had stayed in the Brewster Lodge and I didn't drink or use drugs. He went on to explain that it was considered a dry shelter and that they did random drug tests.

He gave me a form to fill out and began telling me how many nights I could stay. Guests were allowed only six nights at the shelter and then three days out before they could return. He went through my backpack to check out what I had in it. There were only clothes, a toothbrush, shampoo—stuff like that. He then told me to follow him.

We walked down a corridor into what looked like the main congregation room in a church. There were no pews; there were only bunk beds. The lighting was very dim, so I really couldn't tell if the place was clean. The mattresses were the same kind they used at the Brewster: thin, covered with green plastic—standard, institutional mattresses. They weren't the most comfortable, but I was extremely tired and just wanted to sleep. All I needed to do was collect my sheets and make my bed.

I was finally able to get the name of the guy who signed me in: John. He seemed to snap at everyone. But being very tired, I was willing to roll with the punches just to get some sleep. If anyone was snoring, I didn't hear it. I slept soundly.

Everyone had to be out of the building by eight. The first thing I asked in the morning was if there was any coffee around. Some guy pointed toward the hallway and told me they served breakfast in the TV room. I'd seen better continental breakfasts at roadside motels. Dry cereal, orange Kool-Aid, and coffee. They couldn't even get the coffee right. It tasted as bad as the coffee at the Brewster.

I went back to my bed, gathered my things, and headed out the door. I had a Starbucks card with enough money on it to get a decent cup of joe. I nursed that cup of coffee as long as I could, just to stay inside from the cold.

Certain traits of my personality were emerging that proved to be beneficial in times like these. Being able to speak up was one of them. Wandering around Central Square, I saw someone I recognized from the Brewster. "Hey, Robert," I said. We shook hands, and he asked me what I was doing there. I told him I was staying over at Ally's.

"Yeah, me too," he said. Robert was going through some tough times himself.

I said, "Ally's is a dump, huh?"

Robert, with his heavy Jamaican accent, just replied, "You have to do what you have to do, mon. It's better than sleeping on the streets."

Just then some other people started to come around us. Some of them, I noticed, were also staying at Ally's. We introduced ourselves. I asked if they served dinner over at Ally's. "Yeah, about four thirty. Nothing to write home about, but it's hot."

There was a broad array of conversations happening at the same time. Everyone had a complaint about Ally's. Everyone except Robert. We were standing outside of a McDonald's, and a manager didn't like us congregating in front of the place. A couple of the guys were arguing over where the MIT property line ended on Mass Av. Since it was a battle of wits, I could see the conversation was going no place. My brain was pushing out words to babble on with these guys, but my mind was saying, "What the hell am I doing here?"

***

It was two in the afternoon on Saturday, cold but sunny. I only had two bucks to my name, and I was hoping that Labor Force would have some work for me the next week. Oh, how sweet it is! I was stuck there in Central Square in Cambridge for the whole weekend.

I didn't have to get back to the shelter until seven thirty, so I had some time to kill. I thought I'd walk to Harvard Square, which is about a mile from Central Square. With only a couple of dollars, I was willing to stand outside with a cup in my hand and ask for spare change, but it appeared I wasn't the only cup shaker in town. Most of the people standing and bumming change were doing it for food. It was sad to see so many people in that way.

I wanted to do something different besides just stand there with a cup in my hand, so I found a good-sized piece of cardboard and made a sign. My car was still in need of repair, so I simply wrote, "Need Funds $$ to have my radiator replaced on my car in order to get a job."

I found a good spot to put my sign. I didn't have to say a word; people could clearly see it walking by in either direction. I'd just set my cup right in front of my sign and stand there.

A man coming out of one of the shops walked toward me and put what looked like a bundle of ones into the cup. I thanked him. Wow! People *are* sympathetic to my car problem!

It seemed like for every four or five persons who walked by, someone would put something in my cup. I couldn't believe I was doing it, and the only thing I regretted was that I didn't have a bigger cup.

After about two hours, I'd had enough. I didn't do too badly—a grand total of fifty-eight dollars. If the weather had been better, I might have stood out there a little longer. It was hardly enough to replace the radiator in my car, but it was a new experience for me nevertheless.

It was degrading. There's no nice way of putting it. It left a bad taste in my mouth.

***

The people who bum change on a day-to-day basis have probably been down and out for quite a long time and have run out of options. But nobody should go hungry. There are plenty of food banks, food pantries, and soup kitchens, and there are many people who partake of these establishments. Most towns have food pantries that open for business once or twice a week. I'm astonished at the number of people who rely on these food dispensaries just to keep from starving to death.

Being homeless really gave me an up-close look at the reality of what poor people have to deal with every day—so many people whose lives are in disarray. And if you let it overwhelm you emotionally, you end up as broken and confused as they are.

If there was any chance of me pulling out of my crisis, I knew I was only going to do it with perseverance and determination. It was *my* homeless problem, and I would do whatever I felt necessary to pull myself out of it. Contending with homelessness also requires interacting with the homeless. There were so many times when I was inspired by a simple conversation with someone. We worked off one another; *we needed each other.*

***

I was at a point in my life where it seemed the only people I associated with were homeless. Sitting on a park bench looking at the Charles River seemed to be the theme of the month for me.

One day in the park, I met a small group of young adults. I would estimate their ages as being between twenty-two and thirty-five. We introduced ourselves, and the first thing I noticed was how friendly and polite they were. One of them played guitar and loved rock music. And with my musical background, we made an immediate connection and began chatting. It didn't take long for me to find out that all of them were homeless.

More people were showing up, so the group was getting larger. Altogether I saw about nine people. It was apparent that they all knew each other very well and were good friends. One of them told me they had forged a strong bond during the previous winter. Staying together as a group and each one having the other's back, they had looked out for each other.

They had been through very hard times. But all of them seemed to be smart and articulate and appeared to have what it takes to free themselves from homelessness. Whether they did or not, only time would tell.

***

This begs a question: do people living in dire circumstances at the bottom of the economic ladder exhibit a truer definition of what we all can relate to—that is, friendship? If you took the same nine people living on their own in separate dwellings, would they show the same kind of friendship toward each other? In other words, can hard times make you a better person?

Yeah, life isn't always fair. We all know this. But it keeps getting harder just to keep up the pace. Staying afloat in an economic system like ours is no easy task. We always hear how the cost of living is constantly going up. Becoming homeless has made me realize more than ever how expensive living today can be.

It certainly takes a lot of money to exist, let alone live well. You either have it or you don't. I got mine, so you go get yours. It's a free-for-all out there. In a society where this dog-eat-dog mindset flourishes, you're sometimes going to see the negative effects explode on the evening news. For every action, there is an equal and opposite reaction.

I don't claim to have the answers, but I'd like to see our society treat all people in a more dignified manner as we go forth in the twenty-first century. We should be leaps and bounds ahead of the great civilizations of the past as far as providing basic human care, and in some respects, we are. However, we still hear people crying out with their all-too-familiar woes, just as they did back then.

***

Over the intercom system at Ally's, someone announced, "It's snack time." That sounded good! Climbing down from my bunk, I was thinking a snack would hit the spot before I retired for the evening. When I walked into the TV room, there were a couple of people standing in line in front of a metal table. John, who was the senior staff worker during the week, was carrying a large metal bowl and what looked like a loaf of bread. He walked to the table and set it down.

"Are these the snacks?" I asked one of the guests.

"Yup!" he replied.

Are you kidding me? What the hell is this! A bowl of bruised fruit and bread with mold on it. Come on! I wanted to complain, but I held back. I could not believe that this was the best they could do.

It was obvious to me that the staff didn't care whether anyone took advantage of the snacks or not. Looking around the room, I could see that most of the guests were eating snacks that they'd brought from outside the shelter.

It might seem petty to complain about the snacks this shelter provided for the guests, but to me it was not a small issue. Inedible fruit and moldy bread? Hard-core criminals in prison were accommodated better. The shelter wasn't very presentable either. Forget using the bathrooms. They were awfully dirty.

I wanted to ask the staff for an extra blanket, but I really didn't feel like dealing with them.

The main lights were turned off at nine. As I got back to my bunk, I was thinking, *Gee! Having a place to lie down with a roof over your head is really all you need in the first place, isn't it? So, what's the beef?*

Before coming here, I had been under the impression that it was run by a very well-funded organization, and thus I would be well taken care of. However, that wasn't the case.

And the staff was at times contemptuous of the guests. But, to be fair, there was one staff person who was really cool with everyone. He had a very cordial approach. He reassured me that I would have a bed for the night.

That's the way it should be. I mean, not to have your dignity ripped from underneath you. It's too bad that all of the staff weren't like this guy.

***

It was my sixth and therefore my last day at Ally's, so the next morning I had to be out. I needed to find some other place to stay for three days before I could return to the shelter. I wanted to be close to where I worked, so it looked like I'd be heading to Waltham early in the morning. Not knowing where I was going to stay, I guessed I'd have to make it up as I went.

I walked up Mass Av to catch the bus to Watertown, thinking that the buses started rolling at five in the morning, and I wanted to be the first one through the door at Labor Force. I seriously needed to make some money that week.

Not having a place to stay once I got to Waltham added a lot more stress to an already stressful situation for me.

"Morning, Kenny," I said. "Hope I can get some work today."

"Sign in, Jim," Kenny said. "I got something for you."

"Great!" I exclaimed. I signed my name and went to make some coffee for all the early morning folks who might like some too.

My cell phone rang. It was Alex, the guy who was letting me keep my car in his driveway. "Hello, Alex. What are you doing calling me this early in the morning?"

"Jim, you have to get your car out of here today. My wife says the car has to go. I can't do any more for you, Jim."

"That's okay, Alex. I knew this day would be coming. Listen, I'm just unloading a truck today for Labor Force. I'll be finished at noon. Can you meet me at Labor Force and take me back to your place?"

Alex replied, "Okay, Jim, I'll see you then."

I didn't have a clue where my car was going to go. My only hope was that Alex had AAA. As far as where my car was going to be towed, I had to call my mechanic, Dominic.

As I looked in my wallet to find Dominic's phone number, I was extremely worried I wouldn't have a place to store my car until I came up with the money to have it repaired. Dominic already knew the problem with my car; we had talked about it on the phone. Whether or not he would allow my car to stay at his shop while I came up with the money was up to him.

"Hello, Dominic. It's Jim. I'm having my car towed to your shop today. Go ahead and do what you have to do to fix it. I'm not sure if I will have all the money when the job is done. I need at least a couple of weeks before I know how much money I'll have."

Dominic seemed to understand my situation. He told me that was fine and that I could call him in a couple of weeks. I thanked him and hung up.

If I'm able to pull this one off, I'll be one lucky guy!

It was noon, and I was at Labor Force, picking up my check. I looked over my shoulder through the window and saw Alex pulling up. I immediately went outside to greet him.

"Hey, Alex, do you have triple A?" I asked, my fingers crossed.

He responded, "Yes, I do."

"Well, here's the thing. I have a place where the car can be towed, but I don't have triple A. Can you have it towed using your card?"

Alex lowered his head and said, "Well, we have to get the car out of there, so I guess I'll have to."

I couldn't believe he was helping me. What a guy!

After we got the car towed, I told him I would be okay. I was able to hop on a bus from his place and head back to Waltham.

I was determined to hold on to my car, no matter what. I really missed driving it. I'd come up with the money, but it would probably take more than a couple of weeks. I hoped Dominic would help me out and let me keep the car there a bit longer.

***

Sitting on the bus heading back to Waltham, I thought, *Where in the hell am I going to sleep tonight?* It was the afternoon, sunny but cold. I knew I would be dining at the soup kitchen. Maybe I'd run into someone who knew a good spot to hunker down for the night.

I wasn't taking it too bad. It helped to know I'd be working the next day, making some money. The library was open, so I thought I'd go check on the Internet and try to find a second job. I was going to need more than Labor Force wages if I expected to get my car back and put it on the road.

Getting off the bus, I saw somebody I recognized, but I forgot his name.

"Hey, how are you doing? Jim, right?" he exclaimed.

"Yeah, that's right. You're Manny, aren't you?" I replied. I always felt better when I remembered someone's name. Manny had stayed at the Brewster when I was there.

"So, what's up? Still at the Brewster?" I asked.

"Yeah, still there."

Manny was on a long list waiting for subsidized housing. It seemed like he'd been waiting forever. He told me he'd been waiting for more than a year and a half and hadn't heard anything from the housing people yet.

As Manny was talking, I thought of an article I'd read on the Internet about a local politician who was pushing to make housing available for displaced and/or homeless people. Local politicians say a lot of things, but the reality is, you get on a list and then you're pretty much forgotten about. The percentage that gets lucky is so low that it isn't even worth mentioning. Besides, you'd probably end up in a neighborhood that you wouldn't want to live in.

Manny mentioned to me that it was important for me to get a document in writing that confirmed I was homeless. I told him that I didn't see how having a piece of paper about my current living situation would do me any good. But he was persistent and told me that I'd be better off if I had it. He explained that if I wanted to apply for subsidized housing, I would need it.

I called a social worker with the City of Cambridge who dealt with the problems of homeless, displaced, and abused people. I showed up at her office. She introduced herself and asked me to sit down. Then she asked me a series of questions about my current living situation. I explained that I had been homeless for nine months and how tough things were.

Connie was very understanding and sympathetic to the situation that I was confronted with. She went on to say that she heard that kind of story all day long. She also said that I would be shocked at how many people had a similar story.

Walking out of the office after talking to Connie, I had mixed emotions. There I was, spilling my guts to a complete stranger. But oddly it made me feel better to get it off my chest.

***

As I arrived in Waltham, I noticed Richard walking far ahead of me. He was a permanent fixture on the streets around there. I figured he might know of a place where I could sleep that night and that he'd be at the soup kitchen. I'd ask him then.

I saw a lot of familiar faces at the kitchen. It was a pretty good crowd. The food was good, and the people who prepare and serve it seemed to enjoy what they were doing. That was good! Otherwise poor slobs like us would go hungry.

I didn't have anything to lose asking Richard if he knew of someplace I could crash for the night. After dinner, I walked over to his table; he always sat at the same table.

"Hello, Richard. Are you going out to have a cigarette?" I asked. "I want to talk to you for a minute or two."

Richard responded, "Okay, I just want to finish my dessert. It's pretty good tonight."

"Go ahead," I told him.

Richard's voice was very rough and raspy. You really had to pay attention to him when he spoke, or you would miss a lot of what he was saying. Before he could get two words out, I interrupted him. Not wasting time, I told him I was sleeping in the street, and asked if he knew of a good place in town where I could sleep.

"You're not at the Brewster?" Richard responded.

"No, no. I'm not at the Brewster. I'm doing my thirty days out."

He began talking about some park benches at the railroad station across from the Waltham common. I interrupted. "Any other places you might know of? I'm not too keen about sleeping on park benches."

He went on to mention a little hut in the middle of a parking lot behind one of the main banks. It used to be an old train-monitoring booth, but it hadn't been used for many years and was just left abandoned.

Richard went on to explain that I wouldn't be able to lie down once I was inside, because the space was very small. He also added that I would have to wiggle the door handle to open the door. Something was wrong with the lock.

Richard was a very good human being, but you could tell he was a lonely man. He would still be talking to you even though the conversation was over. You could be half a block away, and he'd still be talking, holding his hand to the side of his mouth, like someone would do when whispering into someone's ear.

My conversation with Richard wasn't very helpful. He didn't seem to know too many places where I could crash.

Someone did tell me about a Dunkin' Donuts that was open twenty-four hours. It was right off Main Street, and he told me that he had slept there one night and no one bothered him.

I was going to give that a try. I figured it was best to go there as late as I could. Once inside, I'd buy a small coffee, nurse the hell out of it, and then sack out.

***

I couldn't believe it. I was standing in front of Labor Force casually telling a friend who I hadn't known for long that I'd slept at a Dunkin' Donuts the night before. I was telling him that they had no benches, just chairs. So I had to sit upright and lay my head on a table. It wasn't much of a sleep, but the people who worked the night shift were pretty cool about it.

My friend just had a blank expression on his face as he nodded slightly.

Oh boy! The company I'm keeping these days. I mean, nothing fazes them. I could have told him I slept on some railroad tracks last night, and he would still have the same expression, one of indifference.

I had to work a full day feeling tired. And to make matters worse, I wasn't sure where I was going to sleep that night. And I had to repeat that process for two more nights before I'd be able to go back to Ally's.

Dominic, the mechanic who had my car, called to let me know that the repairs were finished. He also told me the cost for the work done: just over a grand.

I had to do some fast talking and beg Dominic to let me make the payments in installments—a little each week. Understanding that my situation was quite dire, he agreed to work with me.

"Thank you, Dominic," I replied.

I was so relieved I still had my car. Wow! Talk about walking a tightrope.

Saving money to pay for my car repair was a priority. But working at Labor Force, it would take forever to pay it off, especially the way I blew through money. I'd been looking on the Internet, hoping to find a second job, but not having much luck on that front. Not having a car was making it next to impossible to find more work.

I was working with Matt, who I knew from the Brewster. We were cleaning out a store in a mall—a pretty easy gig. The last thing you wanted to be labeled at Labor Force was a *slacker*. Nobody wanted to be sent on a work assignment with someone who didn't share the workload. When you're teamed up with another worker, you want him to be assured that you'll do your share of the work. So there I was, dead tired. No excuses though—I still had to perform. Anyone has to admire the blue-collar work ethic.

At the end of the day, Matt and I picked up our checks and headed out the door. He was in a hurry and said that he needed to catch the bus, something to do with his family.

"Sure, Matt. I'll see you tomorrow."

I figured I'd get something to eat and hang around and think about where I was going to sleep that night. I was thinking about the benches down at the train station. But they were very uncomfortable. You couldn't stretch out, because every five feet there was a big metal armrest that got in your way.

I had another place in mind, but that would mean I'd be sleeping on cold concrete. But I remembered that a long-time street person had told me that if you ever plan to sleep outside, make sure you put a piece of cardboard underneath you rather than sleeping directly on the concrete. He mentioned that it gets pretty cold at night.

It was starting to get dark out, and as I was walking around, my attention was on all the windows throughout the city with their lights coming on—hundreds of them. It reminded me that on the other side of those bright little squares were people, warm and snug, enjoying all the amenities that a home has to offer. But I didn't make the mistake of dwelling on the way things used to be. You can't. To have any chance of surviving this ordeal, you accept the fact that you're homeless and get on with your life.

I had the unpleasant task of locating a piece of cardboard. It had to be big enough that my entire body would be protected from the concrete. I was glad it was dark out. I'd hate to be walking down the street, carrying a big piece of cardboard during the day. I mean, what would I say if someone were to ask me, "What are you going to do with that piece of cardboard?" I guess I could have said, "This isn't a piece of cardboard. It's my mattress!"

The place where I was planning to sleep had a roof over the concrete, which would protect me if it rained. (See the following photo.) The temperature was expected to be in the low forties, which wasn't too bad. My backpack would have to double as my pillow. I had no blanket, just the clothes I was wearing.

I must have been extremely tired, as I slept most of the night. But when I awoke in the early morning, I was freezing my ass off. The old-timer had been right. The cardboard made a difference. And somehow, I'd gotten through it.

Then came my third and final night out on the streets. The weather was overcast; it already felt chilly. Rain would really make it nasty out. I didn't want to go back to Dunkin' Donuts and sleep there again or spend another night on the cold concrete. One more night, and I'd be able to go back to Ally's.

I knew of a van that looked abandoned. It was behind a gas station off Main Street. I'd have to wait until night to check that possibility out.

I was cold. I decided to go have a coffee at Dunkin' Donuts and wait till it was safe to check out the van. Maybe I'd be able to sleep in a dry place.

It was getting close to eleven o'clock—time for me to explore the van. As I approached the building where the van was, I noticed that I'd have to walk under a light that lit up the side of the building. But the van itself was in the back in an unlit area. I walked into the light, hoping no one would see me.

Where I had to spend a couple of nights when there was no other place to go.

Once at the van, I moved around to the back of it. Luckily for me, it was unlocked. It was just a matter of opening the back door, climbing inside, and shutting the door behind me. Amazingly, there was a mattress inside. Obviously I wasn't the first homeless person to have this idea. This was very cool! I was able to stretch out on a mattress and stay dry for the night. But I knew I would be screwed if I overslept in the morning. I needed to be up before sunrise because I didn't want anyone to see me exiting the van.

***

I never would have thought I'd be happy to get back to Ally's. The three days where I was literally living on the streets proved to be pretty rough.

But I was feeling bummed out about having to go back. It was quite far from my work. It took two buses to go from Cambridge to Waltham. But then I had to be back at the shelter in Cambridge by seven thirty. I didn't want to risk losing my bed at Ally's, so having dinner at the soup kitchen in Waltham at five was too risky.

This was my life. And man, I hated it!

I had only a hundred dollars. And I'd blow through that in no time, mostly on food alone. Living was expensive. It didn't care if you were homeless or not.

I was finally at Ally's, going through the usual sign-in procedure. And I was recognizing some familiar faces already. I liked that. I saw a lot of people from the Brewster who also came to Ally's when they were doing their thirty days out.

As I walked into the TV room, I was approached by Mike, a fellow who I knew from Labor Force and the Brewster. "Hey, Jim. How are you doing? Did you get a bed for tonight?"

"Sure did," I responded.

Mike asked me if I had a cigarette. He also quickly mentioned that he had only two more nights there. And he wasn't sure where he was going to go next.

Someone yelled, "Smoke break!"

Mike wanted to know if I was going to go outside for a butt.

"Yes," I replied. "Oh, here's a cigarette."

Mike thanked me. We went outside to shoot the bull and have a smoke. I asked him if he'd been to Labor Force lately. He told me his bus card had no money on it, so he wasn't able to take the bus anywhere.

Conversations, for the most part, usually stayed away from our homeless predicament. And we ended up just talking about anything irrelevant to pass the time. But Mike seemed interested in what I was doing and where I was staying.

I simply told him that I'd just signed in there for six more nights. And hopefully I'd get back into the Brewster in ten days.

I also mentioned to him that I was literally living in the streets when I wasn't there at Ally's. I added that I tried to stay close to Labor Force when I wasn't there.

He nodded and said, "Yeah, yeah." He told me that he had to get to Labor Force soon because he had no money.

I wasn't in any position to lend him money, so I just shook my head and told him, "I know. Things are tight." Who else could I expect to run into at a homeless shelter but people like Mike: desperate, no money, and who knows what else?

It was getting close to bedtime. Some people were watching a hockey game on TV. I was just sitting by myself, thinking about things. Somebody had provided me the opportunity to sleep in a warm bed rather than my only other option: the streets. And for that, I was very grateful.

But why did we need a curfew—to be in by a certain time and not be able to leave the shelter until the next morning? We were all adults. And, as such, we should be allowed to take care of ourselves and be responsible. Having that kind of respect from the higher-ups in a homeless shelter would say to the guests that they are being treated like normal people despite their homeless status. Their freedom should not be compromised. And why should it? For simply being homeless?

I recognize that there have to be rules for everyone to follow. A shelter without rules would be chaos. But when people are told when they can come or go—well, that's all it really takes for them to realize that *they don't want to be there.* And they will find a way to right the ship.

I wonder if the people who run shelters use this as reverse psychology to push homeless people to get back on their feet.

A suggested place for homeless people to sleep out of the rain.

***

The next day I was up early and out the door, heading to Labor Force. It was discouraging working for only eight dollars an hour. But at that point, it was all I had. Man, I needed to step it up and find a better working situation.

As I was signing in, someone tapped me on the shoulder. It was Doug. I wasn't too familiar with him, but I did know he had a car.

"What's up?" I said.

"You're coming with me. Nice job, right here in town," Doug explained. Then one of the Labor Force managers mentioned that it was a full day.

"Sounds good to me," I responded.

The job started at seven thirty. I had plenty of time to go have a coffee, so I walked across the street to Starbucks. I met Matt on the way. "Hey, dude! Good morning!" I exclaimed.

"Where are you staying?" Matt asked.

"I'm still over at Ally's, living the good life."

Matt laughed and said, "Yeah, I've been there too. What a hole!"

"Yeah, Matt. But at least it's dry inside."

"You getting a coffee?"

"Yes."

Matt and I were sitting at a table, sipping our coffee, when I said that I'd be back at the Brewster in a week or so. Knowing Matt was currently staying at the Brewster, I asked, "How are things going there?"

"Oh, same old shit. Everyone's tripping over each other."

"This time Robbie is sure to give me a urine test," I said. "So I need to stay clean."

After responding to Matt's questions about what was going on in my life, I began to rant about Marie over at Labor Force. "Who in the hell does Marie think she is anyway, huh? I want to tell her, will you just give me my work assignment and *stay out of my personal life?*"

It's funny how people want to know what's happening in your life. Has any break come your way? What sort of work are you doing? And so on. Nothing changes. It was just as it had been before I became homeless. People still played the "keeping up with the Joneses" game—even way down at the bottom of the economic ladder.

"Having a problem with Marie, eh?" Matt said.

"I don't think the people over there should nose into our private affairs. She's telling me that I should have enough money saved up by now to pay for my auto repair. And she doesn't even know how much it will actually cost me. She's only guessing."

Matt replied, "Jim, you know where they're coming from. They just want another car so they can pile some more people in and send them off to jobs. It's all about their bottom line."

"Of course, Matt. I know you're right. But where do they get off telling you what to do with your money? I wanted to say to her, 'Marie, please mind your own business and *stay out of mine!*' But I bit my tongue instead. You know if you say anything to piss them off, they'll send you out on even lousier jobs."

I started questioning myself. Was I not entitled to run my own affairs anymore? Did people think they could kick me around simply because I was homeless?

As Matt got up and headed to the door, he mentioned to me that I think too much.

"Bullshit!" I responded. "This is really happening. She's paying too much attention to my business. I can't believe some people. They really put up with this kind of abuse. It's like people just give up. They simply don't care anymore. They lose their fight."

When Matt and I returned to Labor Force, Marie told me my job assignment had changed. I was going to Burlington with Walter and some other dude I didn't even know.

After getting our work tickets from Marie, we piled into the car and took off. We introduced ourselves and talked about the job we were heading to. Everyone seemed to agree that it would be a decent gig.

Sitting in the back seat, I noticed that Kyle was pulling out a blunt (marijuana rolled in a tobacco leaf). Walter smiled and said to Kyle, "Do it up! Do it up!" Then he asked me if I wanted to smoke some.

I told him, "I can't. I'm going to be checking back into the Brewster. And I'll have to do a urine test for sure this time." My eyes were starting to water. They were smoking some good stuff. It smelled *very* potent.

I laughed and said to them, "I hope I don't get a contact high."

But who was I kidding? I was going to be riding to and from work all week with these guys. And if they kept it up, I wasn't going to pass my urine test, which was in three days. This was a true case of being between a rock and a hard place. I needed to earn some money, but I also very much wanted to get back into the Brewster.

I could have asked Walter if he wouldn't mind waiting until we got to work to get high. That way I wouldn't be breathing secondhand smoke from their little marijuana session. But it was his car, and I felt I had no right to suggest that to him.

For a second I thought maybe Robbie would give me a break and not test me. *Yeah, right. As if that's going to happen.*

The work turned out to be more like hard labor. The mall store we were working at had just gone out of business. And our job was to dismantle it. It was a good-sized store with a lot of counters that needed to be broken down and carted outside. Typical Labor Force grunt work.

It was the end of the day, and I just wanted to get back to Ally's and sleep, sleep, sleep. I was standing outside the shelter, getting ready to go in, when I noticed that the second door, which went into the area where you sign in, was ajar. It was usually locked, and you would wait for a staff member to let you in.

I decided to just walk in anyway and sign in. All of a sudden, some staff guy started in on me, yelling at me and asking me why didn't I wait until a staff member let me in. He was very angry. I thought he was way out of line and didn't need to scream at me. For every little offense around there, it seemed that those guys enjoyed yelling at us.

I knew something was wrong with that kind of behavior. We weren't confrontational, we were homeless! Why did staff members have to jump in our faces like it was some kind of street fight? We weren't there for a fight; we were homeless. We didn't need anybody snapping in our face. *It just wasn't right!*

I hoped more than ever that I'd be back at the Brewster. The next day I was up at five and out the door.

***

I usually felt positive about things working out. But I had a bad feeling about passing the urine test. I was stressed out with thoughts of what I was going to do if the test came back positive.

Things were not going as planned. I was running late to do my intake with Robbie. I wanted to be at the shelter before the other guests arrived. That way I would have a one-on-one with Robbie. In other words, I would have his undivided attention.

But that isn't what happened. All the regulars were starting to pile in. Walking up the stairs, I saw some familiar faces from my previous stay there at the Brewster.

"Hey, Jim. How are things? Are you coming back to this place?" they asked.

And I replied, "Yeah, that's the plan."

Once at the top of the stairs, I turned to go to the office. There was Robbie. "Hello, James. Are you here for your intake?"

"Yes, I am," I responded.

"Okay, just a second. I need to get some forms for you to fill out. By the way, James, this time I will need a urine sample from you."

"Yeah, I figured as much," I said.

After filling out the forms, Robbie handed me a container, which I was supposed to piss in. I took the container and went into the bathroom. I thought it was strange that Robbie was following me into the bathroom. Walking to the urinal, I noticed that Robbie was right behind me, making sure that I was actually peeing into the container.

I turned and asked Robbie, "Why are you standing there?"

"Never mind me," he replied. "Just go ahead and pee into the container."

This was my first time having to take a urine test, and it was concerning to me that somebody would want to watch me pee in a cup.

Robbie explained to me as we walked back to the office that he was required to be present in the bathroom. He said that some people cheat when doing a urine test. They could have someone without drugs in their urine pee in the cup. Or they could bring in a container with "clean" urine, and put it into the cup.

I was starting to get a little nervous. Robbie tried to calm me down and told me it would take a couple of minutes to get the result. The plastic container had a strip on the inside that changed color if the urine sample contained alcohol or drugs.

Robbie held the cup up and said, "It doesn't look good." The strip was starting to change color. Robbie told me that the test showed a large concentration of THC (a chemical found in marijuana).

"What does this mean?" I said to Robbie.

"Sorry, James, but you're not going to be able to stay here tonight. And you won't be able to come back and be retested for two weeks."

"Great! Now what I am going to do? I don't have anyplace to go."

Robbie explained that his superiors were watching his every move. I could tell that he felt bad, but he had no choice. He had to stick with the shelter's policy. It was a dry shelter after all, so they didn't allow any guest to consume alcohol or use drugs.

I started to make a ruckus in the office. Feeling extremely upset and desperately needing a place to stay, I pleaded with Robbie to let it go this time and let me stay. Then his boss walked in. She had been appointed a month before as head of the Brewster Lodge. She asked Robbie, "What seems to be the problem here?"

Robbie told her that my urine test was positive.

She said, "There's not much we can do. Sorry, those are the shelter's rules. There are other shelters that you can go to. Robbie can give you a list of them." Then she went on to suggest, "Have you ever been to the Pine Street Inn?"

That's when I looked at her, and if eyes could kill, she would have been a goner. I screamed, "Are you kidding me? That filthy place? I don't think so! (The Pine Street Inn was a wet shelter that let *anybody* in.)

I grabbed my things and stormed out, telling Robbie that I'd be back in two weeks.

4

THE HOMELESS AND THE LIVING

It was the beginning of March, cold and rainy. I was standing at a bus stop, waiting to take a bus back to Ally's, when an old bag lady walked up. She watched me open a fresh pack of cigarettes and asked me if I could spare one.

"Sure, here you go," I said.

Turning away, I looked up the street to see if the bus was coming. Another person waiting at the bus stop overheard me mumbling that I wished that the bus would hurry up and come. He responded, "I have to get home too. My dinner's waiting."

Then the old bag lady said, "Home, huh? I wish I had a home to go to."

I didn't say anything. I just stood there silent, waiting for the bus. The old lady kept talking about how hard it is to be homeless. I wanted to say something to her—anything—to make her feel better, maybe give her some hope. But I just stood there saying nothing until the bus finally pulled up.

As I stepped onto the bus, she seemed to direct her frustration at me and let out what I can only describe as a desperate cry, as if she were having a mental breakdown. Just as the door closed behind me, she cried out with a gravelly, horrible-sounding voice, "Being homeless is a *nightmare!*"

The sound of her voice and how she said it resonated through my head as I was looking for a place to sit on the bus. It was as if she purposely wanted me to hear her in her time of despair.

Sometimes I can be very impressionable. I was obviously sensitized by the whole encounter. All I could think about on the bus ride back to the homeless shelter at Ally's was that old lady crying out for help. Why she chose that time and place to do so I'll never know.

But what the hell could I do? There were shelters just for women in the area, probably where she was staying.

But that sounds like one of those convenient answers served on a silver platter for those who will never in their lifetime become homeless. There *are* shelters for homeless women. The majority of people are satisfied with that response. I wasn't any different before I became homeless. But, boy, did I see it in a whole new light now that I too had become homeless.

That poor woman had lost her will to fight a long time before that day. And the only thing left for her was to go on suffering terribly in her own private homeless purgatory.

If anybody needs an example of what happens the longer someone remains homeless, there are plenty of people like her to keep reminding us what's at stake.

***

I was standing in front of the homeless shelter, talking to some shelter guests about the newly renovated shelter that would open soon. It would be a step up from what it was now. Finally, it was nice to hear that some of the money donated to that international organization was being put to some good use.

But that being said, I hoped I'd never have to use the new facility. I wasn't the least bit interested in a newly renovated homeless shelter. I wanted to run as far away as I could from places like that.

Man, it was tough out there! At times, there was a little too much humanity for my liking. Even though I detested it so, there was an amount of acceptance that I had to yield to. Homelessness could consume you, swallow you whole, whether you wanted to believe it or not.

Before going back inside, I was finishing up a conversation with one of the guests there at Ally's. We had a disagreement as to whether or not the homeless shelter's new addition would make a difference. I went on to say that the numbers of available beds at the new facility weren't even worth mentioning in comparison to the number of homeless people in the greater Boston area. There simply aren't enough shelters to meet the demand.

In the time that I had been homeless, I'd come to a realization that society as a whole says to the homeless, "Sorry, but there's not much we can do for you."

But that sounds right to me. There are no guarantees in life, and that includes owning a home, renting an apartment, or living as a boarder. Places to live don't just appear out of thin air. These kinds of things take work and action—that is, if you aren't the beneficiary of a large inheritance. I don't think that people who become homeless expect someone to hand them a home, but I do feel that providing adequate shelter to the homeless is essential.

***

It was just getting to be evening at Ally's, and someone mentioned getting some coffee. That sounded good to me. Walking over to the coffee dispenser to grab a Styrofoam cup, I, like everyone else around there, knew that the coffee wasn't any good. A few comments were tossed around about the lousy coffee, but still everyone waited their turn to get some.

I asked who was responsible for making the coffee. That's when someone tapped me on the shoulder and pointed to one of the guests. I said, "*That* guy?" He was very dirty and grimy. He didn't look like anyone who cared whether you had a good-tasting cup of coffee.

I turned and said to the guy who pointed him out that we'd be better off getting someone else to make the coffee. He nodded.

"Hey, Jim, how are you doing, you ol' malcontent?"

I turned to see John, a friend I'd met through the job agency. I asked him what he was doing here.

"It's a long story," he replied.

"Aren't they all?" I said.

I remembered him telling everyone how good things were going for him only two weeks before. But his girlfriend had thrown him out. He told me that he knew he had taken a risk going back to live with her.

I'd known John only for a short time, but he was a good guy and a hard worker. I felt sorry for him for being tossed out on the street. I looked over at him and noticed that he seemed agitated about something. I asked him, "Is everything okay?"

Instead of answering, he asked, "How is it here at this shelter?"

"Well, it sure isn't home by any stretch of the imagination," I replied. "But you get a dry bunk and a roof overhead to keep the rain off you. Oh, let's see … the coffee sucks, and they serve dinner at four thirty every day. I've never made it back here in time to partake, so I can't tell you if it's any good. You get six nights in, and then you have to be out for three nights before you can come back. You have to be back here in the evening by no later than seven thirty, or take the risk that you lose your bed." Then I asked, "Is this the first time you've been in a homeless shelter?"

"Yes," he answered.

"Gee, John, talk about a switch in your living situation!" Then I had to ask him, "What do you think about this place so far?"

He looked around the room and said he didn't think he was going to stay the night. He mentioned that he felt uneasy.

"I certainly can understand that," I said. "Myself, I've been homeless for ten months now, and I still have a hard time coming to places like this. But for you, being your first time in a homeless shelter, this must be a real shock to your system."

I was getting tired and ready to hit the sack. But before I did, I mentioned to John that the next day, if the weather was nice, I was going to walk to Harvard Square, and if he wanted to come that would be cool.

He asked me what time in the morning we had to be out by.

"Eight o'clock," I said.

"Okay, I'll catch you in the morning."

"Alright, John, nice talking to you. Good night."

***

The following morning, while everyone was having coffee, I noticed that John *did* stay the night. "Good morning, John," I said. "I see you're still here."

"I guess I was pretty tired," John replied. He asked me what I was going to do that day.

"Well, it's the weekend. I'm just going to hang around this side of town. I was thinking about taking a walk to Harvard Square."

"Do you mind if I tag along?" John asked.

"Not at all. I just have to get my things, and we'll go. It's only a fifteen-minute walk to Harvard Square."

"That's not bad," he said. Then he asked how many times I had been at this shelter.

"Oh, this will be my fourth visit. And I hope it's my last. But the way things are going, it doesn't look that way." I also mentioned that I had a car in Norwood waiting for me to pay off an auto repair. John asked me how much money it was going to cost me. "A little over a grand," I said. "But all in all, I'm starting to adjust better, considering what I'm up against."

"What do you mean, *adjust*?" John asked.

"Don't misunderstand me. I'll never be able to adjust to something like being homeless. I guess what I'm trying to say is that I'm coping better."

If someone was to ask me for an analogy, I would tell them that it's like being able to walk away from a very bad accident.

Part of what I mean when I say I'm adjusting, is that I have to realize that it's going to take time for me to get myself out of homelessness.

I was quite taken by how John seemed very interested in what I was going through. Most conversations with people on the street were just small talk, unrelated to homelessness. But my conversation with John allowed me to talk about what I had been going through.

Turning to John, I said, "I hope you and your girlfriend patch things up so you can get back to a normal life."

"We'll see," John said. "I'm going to call her today to see if she lets me come back."

"Good luck," I said.

***

Another weekend gone, and I was on the bus heading to Waltham, hoping to work a full week. I needed to send some money to Dominic for my car repair.

Looking through my wallet, I found a list of homeless shelters in the greater Boston area that Robbie had given to me. I needed to find a different shelter instead of always depending on Ally's. I was getting sick of that place.

There was one in Harvard Square that looked interesting to me. Students from Harvard University ran it. I thought I'd give them a call in the morning.

It was kind of cool the way people got to that shelter. They did it strictly by lottery. You called them up at seven thirty in the morning, and they gave you a number and told you to call them back in half an hour. If they pulled your number when you called back, you were in.

There was still enough time to make the five o'clock dinner at the soup kitchen in Waltham. I'd heard through the grapevine that they were having pizza, so I knew it was Monday—their usual pizza night. Local pizza establishments donated their pizza to the soup kitchen, so the pizzas were usually pretty good.

I always ran into familiar faces at the soup kitchen. But I didn't have time to mingle at all. I just wolfed down the pizza and headed to the bus stop. I needed to be back at Ally's by seven thirty.

On the bus ride back to Ally's, I was really feeling tired of it all. There was a part of me that rejected all of the charity and standing in line at soup kitchens. After a while, you get so tired of being around it. It had also been a real drag having to depend on the bus to get around.

When I got back to Ally's, all I wanted to do was sleep. I needed to get up early the next day; I had a busy week ahead.

***

It was 7:30 a.m., time for me to call the Harvard University Shelter at the Lutheran Church in Harvard Square. A friendly voice introduced herself. I told her that I was homeless, and I was wondering if I could get into the shelter. She told me that my number was four and to call back in half an hour to see if my number was selected.

Meanwhile, I chatted with Walter from the job agency. We were both working together in Waltham doing some restoration work.

Matt strolled by and asked, "Hey, Jim, how are you doing?"

"Just hanging in there. I'm working in Waltham all this week."

Matt was going out on another job. I told him that I'd catch him later. I then said to Walter that it had been half an hour since I'd called the Harvard Shelter. "Let's see if my number comes up!"

The person who answered the phone asked me if my name was Jim. "Yes," I told her. "I called earlier and was given the number four." She immediately congratulated me and told me that my number came up. I was *so* happy to hear that. She told me that I could come in any time that week to start my two-week stay at the shelter.

"Wow, I got into the shelter! They picked my number!"

Walter smiled at me and said, "That's great."

"You know it!" I said.

That day the work was really hard: knocking down walls and picking up debris and other heavy objects. The day was coming to an end, and I said to Walter that I was looking forward to going to the new shelter.

At four thirty in the afternoon, I was on my way to Harvard Square. I had the address of the church, so I knew where to go.

When I got to the church, I asked someone standing outside if they knew where the entrance to the homeless shelter was. The person pointed to a door. I turned and thanked him and started to walk down the sidewalk to a couple of stairs that led to a set of double doors.

I was greeted by what seemed to be a security guard. He asked me my name and what my business there was. I told him my name was Jim and that I was a new guest at the shelter. He located my name on a clipboard and told me to wait while he went to get someone.

A young woman came up to greet me and welcomed me to the shelter. She said her name was Janet and proceeded to give me the rules for the shelter. She said that the time period of my stay was two weeks, and she began showing me around the shelter. She took me to the dorm room, pointed out my bed, and said that was where I'd be sleeping.

Janet then showed me the kitchen. It was a big one, and adjacent to it was the dining area. "This is where we'll be serving breakfast and dinner—and lunch on the weekends," she said.

She showed me some other rooms then turned and said, "You can watch whatever you want. We have televisions, computers, and a DVD player. And at the end of the hall we have a laundry room where you can do your laundry."

The shelter had a capacity of around twenty people. It was set up to accommodate both men and women.

"Jim," Janet said, "I need to ask you a few questions, and then I'll assign you a locker." She then asked me some simple questions, like my name, date of birth, and my reason for becoming homeless.

After that she went on to explain a few rules. She asked me if I smoked cigarettes. I told her yes, and she said there was a designated place for that, and I could go there any time I wanted. I had to be out by eight in the morning and could get back in as early as four. And on the weekends I could stay in all day.

She also mentioned that all guests got a pair of flip-flops for going in and out of the shower and going back to our room.

The shelter was open from Columbus Day and ran through to the middle of April.

The last thing she explained to me was that they didn't put up with any rowdy behavior, and no drinking or drugs were allowed. The kitchen was always open, and they provided a lot of good food any time you wanted. Normally breakfast was served at seven and dinner at five. And they had real utensils and plates, not just Styrofoam cups and plastic utensils (like at the Brewster, the soup kitchen, and Ally's).

I found the place to be super clean and very comfortable, just like a home would be. Too bad a stay was only for two weeks. It was like a tease.

Lying back on my bed that evening, I was looking around and thinking that, although it was just a token gesture relative to the enormous homeless problem, I still had to applaud the students at Harvard University for at least attempting to address the homeless problem and bringing comfort to some going through it. It was kind of funny, but what this amounted to was nothing more than an all-expense-paid, two-week vacation in lovely Harvard Square, sponsored by Harvard University.

After my shower, I was starving, and it was time for dinner. Right away I was impressed with the amount of food. It really looked good. They gave us as much as we wanted. And the coffee—unlike the other places I'd been—was remarkably good.

After my first week at the Harvard Homeless Shelter, I noticed somebody coming in that I knew from the Brewster. It was Tom.

"Hey, Tom, how ya doing?" I said in greeting. "Welcome to the Harvard shelter! Quite a difference from the Brewster, huh?"

"Sure is! How long have you been here, Jim?" he asked.

"One week so far. It's a very nice place, but the stay is way too short!"

I also mentioned to Tom that the food was great.

There were multiple televisions available to us, so we could view a movie by ourselves if we wanted and sit in a nice, big comfortable chair.

The place was awesome. It really made me think about what I was missing by not having my own place. The young Harvard students who ran it seemed very sincere, and they looked like they were enjoying helping us.

Well, unfortunately my stay at the Harvard homeless shelter was about to end. And it reinforced how much I missed having my own place.

***

Park bench where I spent a lot of time sitting and contemplating.

I was sitting in a coffee shop with Matt. He asked me if I was going to go back to the Brewster. I told him that I was trying to get back in, but I'd failed the urine test twice. "Hopefully the next time I see Robbie, I'll be able to get in."

Matt said that he would also be going back to the Brewster soon. I was explaining to him that it was a pain in the ass staying at Ally's and having to commute to Waltham to work.

One of the younger guys from the Brewster came over to where Matt and I were sitting and asked us if one of us could do him a favor.

"What's the favor?" I asked.

"I need somebody to go to the Baptist Church on Main Street and see if they can get a food voucher for Hannaford's supermarket." (The church provided a fifteen-dollar debit card for food). He went on to explain that the church gave one per person every six months, and he'd already received his.

I said, "If I go to the church to get a food voucher, I'll keep it for myself. I'm not doing that well. I could use some help too."

Matt didn't show any interest in what the guy was saying either.

I turned to Matt and said that I didn't know that the church was giving out food vouchers. He said that he didn't know about it either. I also told Matt I needed to sign up for food stamps. I was getting tired of depending on soup kitchens and food banks.

***

It was Friday afternoon, and I was on my way to see Robbie. This was my third attempt to get into the Brewster. I had called the Brewster earlier that day to see if there were any beds available. They told me there were.

As I walked up the stairs to go see Robbie, I had my fingers crossed.

"Hello, James." Robbie always called me James.

"Hello, Robbie. How are you?" I said.

"Come on in, James. This time I'm *not* going to test you. Just come on in. I'll assign you a bed."

"Oh, thank God! Thank you, Robbie, *thank you!*" I was so relieved.

Robbie knew that I was going through some hard times, and that this time around he just couldn't refuse me. It was just what I needed.

I was feeling hungry, and the only food available were the sandwiches that they kept in the office. They were made every day at the soup kitchen in Waltham and taken to the Brewster so guests would have at least something to eat. The sandwiches were not very good—in fact, they were terrible—but when you're hungry, you'll eat anything.

I was lucky to be in the small dorm room just like the last time I was here. There were fewer people to keep you up with their snoring. I recognized most of the guests. One of the guests, Mike, came over to me and asked, "Where have you been?"

I told him, "I was staying at a homeless shelter in Cambridge Central Square, and I also stayed at the homeless shelter at the Lutheran Church in Harvard Square."

Mike said that he had a friend who also stayed there and said it was a really nice place.

"Yes, it's a very nice place. It's just too bad you're only allowed a two-week stay."

"That's no time at all!" Mike said.

"Right," I said. "How are things here at the Brewster?"

"The same," he said.

***

It was early morning, and I was up and wanting a cup of coffee. But the rule at the shelter was "No making coffee before six." But some of the guests would disregard that policy, so there usually was a pot of coffee brewing for the early morning folks.

A few of the guests started assembling in the kitchen. They were glad to see that someone had made coffee. At a quarter after five a line of people was already standing in front of the coffee pot. Some things will never change. There I was, up to my old stuff, asking someone to watch out for the staff as I slipped out the back door to have a cigarette. Sometimes I took too much of a risk; I knew my butt could be kicked out of the shelter for up to two weeks.

There were four guests and I just sitting around the kitchen table, drinking our coffee. They looked very tired and out of it. It was dead silent in the room. All of a sudden, a strange, poignant vibe engulfed the room. The others seemed to all at once drop their heads to their hands. And, after about five seconds, they simultaneously raised their heads and let out a heavy sigh.

I knew they all were having a real low moment. But the funny thing was that none of them realized they had done it at the same time. It was a really depressing scene to witness.

But at the same time, I felt relief. There at the Brewster, things were familiar to me and consequently gave me a much-needed sense of security. And those days, I'd take all the security I could get. Compared to the six-day time period at Ally's and two weeks at the Harvard shelter, ninety days at the Brewster seemed like real security.

A park where homeless people would often gather

The next day, a friend of mine, also staying at the shelter, gave me a lift to Chelsea so I could apply for food stamps. Just as I had never imagined myself homeless, I never would have thought I'd have to depend on public assistance.

Work was slim to none at Labor Force. I was trying to pay off my auto repair, and that was draining me of all my money. And I was in desperate need of a new pair of boots; my old boots were falling apart.

One of the guests mentioned to me that I could get a clothing voucher for twenty-five dollars to use at the thrift store on Moody Street. He'd gotten a few things there, and he said it wasn't a bad deal at all.

I said to him, "Thanks. I'll give it a try."

It was evening back at the Brewster. I remembered that Robbie had told me he wanted to give me a voucher to get some boots to replace my old ones. I went into the office, and he gave me a twenty-five-dollar voucher to use at a nearby thrift store. Even though the policy was that once you came into the shelter you couldn't leave, Robbie told me he'd give me permission to leave to go to the store and get back in.

I walked to the thrift store. I wasn't going to hold my breath about finding anything decent at that second-hand shop, especially when it came to clothes or shoes. Sure, I'd heard of hand-me-downs growing up, but those were clothes handed down from a family member, not a complete stranger. Nevertheless, no harm in looking.

But the quality of the stuff was so bad and the selection was so poor that I decided none of it was for me—even though I was homeless. The more I looked around, the more disgusted I got, so I just left.

Walking over the bridge, heading back to the Brewster, I was thinking how bad I would feel if I returned the voucher because there was nothing there that I liked. So I turned around and headed back to the thrift store to see if I could find *something* I could use. But to no avail. I hoped Robbie wouldn't think I was ungrateful, especially because he was only trying to help. But the selection there was absolute *garbage*.

When I returned the voucher to Robbie, I just said that I didn't find anything I liked, and thanked him for his offer.

There wasn't any work down at the job agency, and everyone was disappointed to hear that. You can't blame them for being upset. Most of the people got up early in the morning to get down there by five, just to sit around for hours with no work prospects. *That sucks!*

I decided to go to the library and check out what I could find on the Internet as far as employment possibilities. Going to the library was almost like being back at the shelter. It seemed that nearly everyone from the Brewster was there.

Not having my car made it almost impossible to find a job on the Internet. If I couldn't find anything in my general vicinity or accessible by a bus, I would be out of luck.

We were allowed only one hour on the computer before it was someone else's turn to use it. An hour gave me plenty of time to scout around for work and check my email and what not. I usually frequented the library two or three times a day to repeat the process.

I'd always run into someone who would join me in a walk to get a cup of coffee and breakfast at the nearby Salvation Army church. One of the patrons at the church was stirring up controversy by telling everyone that the fresh goods donated to the church didn't make it to the guests, but instead were taken by the staff for their personal use. I really didn't care myself. The coffee was pretty good. So what if the muffins were a day old. The way I figured it, I was happy just to get what they gave out.

The people that worked there were nice enough, and sometimes the woman in the kitchen would make a hot breakfast for everyone. Some days she made sausage and eggs, and it wasn't too bad. Besides, there was always someone to have a good conversation with, talking about what's going on in the world today.

One morning I looked up and saw Matt.

"Hey, Matt, how are you doing?"

"Jim, you sidewinder you! How the hell are you?" he replied.

Matt had some family living in Rhode Island. That's where he went when he got sick of the shelter scene. However, he was never able to stay there for long, because he and his sister hated each other. I guess there's something to that old adage that you can pick your friends but not your family.

"Have you had anything to eat yet?" I asked Matt.

"No. Is there anything good to eat here?" Matt responded.

"They made some sausage and eggs earlier. There might be some left."

As Matt went over to get his food, I talked with Mary, who worked part-time at a retail store in Waltham. She asked me if I'd found any full-time employment yet. I told her I was still looking. I also mentioned to her that not having my car was making it difficult for me.

Mary told me she had recently bought a car and how difficult it was to keep up with car payments, let alone all the other costs that go along with having a car.

"Tell me about it!" I said.

Matt came over, sat down, and started eating his food. He also knew Mary and asked her how things were going.

"Not good," she said. "Sam (her husband) is drinking way too much. And if he keeps it up, I'm going to leave him." Matt and I both knew Sam. He was a good guy but drank like a fish.

Mary said it was time for her to get to work. After she left, I told Matt that if Sam lost Mary, that would be very bad for him. She was a good woman. Matt agreed. I then asked Matt what he was going to do after he'd finished there. He told me he had an appointment with Robbie later on.

"You're coming back to the Brewster?" I asked. "I just got in myself."

After Matt finished eating, we walked over to the convenience store. Every time we get together, we talked about how bad things were and how it would be nice to get a break.

Matt and I were walking down the street when I turned to him and said, "Something will come up. It's the hard part we have to muster. And that is to *hang in there* somehow."

We took turns reminiscing back and forth about how good things used to be. I said, "It's crazy how we've become so attached to material things. Consequently, when we lose them, we feel useless. To keep up the pace in this day and age, we need *things*."

Then, out of the blue, Matt said, "It's a thin line between what is good and what is bad." I wasn't sure what he meant, but I didn't agree with the thin line jazz he was referring to.

"Bullshit, Matt," I said. "There isn't any thin line or safety zone, no place on earth to tread peacefully. From birth to death, we are smack-dab in the middle, torn between temptation and righteousness … Torment, we live in torment."

Matt turned to me and said calmly, "If you had Jesus, there would be no torment."

That was Matt for you. He had a strong religious conviction. That, of course, was fine by me. But I avoided in-depth conversations concerning politics and religion. I tended to keep my spiritual beliefs to myself.

Matt and I would always kid around with each other, simulating the dialect of the old western cowboy. I turned to Matt and said, "Hey, you old saddle-rustler, you!" Matt smiled. But I had no intention of being humorous in what I was about to ask him. "Seriously. What are you going to do? What are your plans, if any?"

Matt had a tired look on his face. Looking down, he said, "I don't know. What about you?"

"My immediate future doesn't look good at all. I dread being stuck in this town all summer long with no car, no foreseeable steady work—and living in a shelter. If there was a time to take a leap of faith, now would be the time to do it."

Rush hour was just starting, and Matt—hunched over—walked slowly to the edge of the sidewalk and said to me, "I wonder how many people out there are just one week or one month away from becoming homeless themselves?"

I responded, "That's a scary thought. I wouldn't wish homelessness on my worst enemy! You know, Matt, something's gotta break for us. Existing like this is for the birds."

Matt says, "Yeah, it sucks. It's like *the homeless and the living.*"

And I said, "I've had enough of this homeless crap. I'm going to rejoin the living … again.

5

HOME STRETCH

Over time, I acquired a lot of skills as a handyman. Since my days in a trade school as a heating and air-conditioning technician, I've also done a lot of work as a building maintenance mechanic. Being a painter is also something I'm good at.

As a result, I landed a position as a handyman in a fifteen-unit apartment building on the outskirts of the city. I get free room and board for my maintenance services. This is a big deal for me, as it got me off the streets and out of homeless shelters.

My living quarters were about the size of a studio apartment, with one bath and a kitchenette. The place suits me fine.

My job and living situation are literally one and the same. In other words, if I don't do my duties for the tenants here at the building, I'll lose my apartment. That isn't a proposition that I'm comfortable with. But I'll have to make do.

I still keep in touch with a couple of the people that I became close friends with during the time I was homeless. You can't help but bond with those who you shared such a miserable time with. They understand what I went through better than anybody else could.

What I endured was traumatic, and I would be lying if I said I bear no resentment. I expect that it will take some time for me to get back to my old self.

One day, my old friend Mike called.

"Hey, Mike, what's up?" I responded.

"Jim, where are you these days? I haven't seen you around."

"I'm just down the street, sort of. I have my own place, and if you're not doing anything right now, you're welcome to stop by."

"That sounds good. Where do you live?"

After giving Mike directions, someone was knocking at my door. One of the tenants needed help moving a piece of furniture from one room to another. It didn't take me any time to do it. Walking back to my unit, I needed to see if I had the right tools for an upcoming landscaping job.

After returning to my apartment, I heard someone else knocking at the door. It was Mike. When I opened the door, he immediately asked me if I was watching the news.

"No, why?" I said.

Mike told me that he was watching television when they interrupted to announce that a bomb had blown up at the Boston Marathon. Hearing that, I looked for the remote to turn the TV on.

It seemed that all the stations were covering the story. Mike also told me that a New York publication blamed the marathon bombing on a "bag man," which was a derogatory term for a homeless person. But it was quickly determined that other suspects were responsible, and the bag man story was tossed.

I chimed in and said, "If things aren't bad enough, now we have crazies that want to blow us up. What's this world coming to?"

Reaching for the remote, I said that we'd be hearing about that story for a long, long time. Turning off the TV, I mentioned to Mike that I might be going to the soup kitchen for supper.

As he was leaving, he told me that he would stop by again, now that he knew where I live.

After Mike left, I decided to go to the library to use a computer and check out a blog that was frequently used by homeless people. There was one person who refused to speak to anyone other than someone who was currently homeless or had experienced it. He wrote on his blog that there is no common ground between someone who has experienced homelessness and someone who has not. He went on to say that people who haven't experienced homelessness don't have a clue what it's like to be in that predicament. I like this guy. He's really cool.

Yet although I understand his position, I think he's absolutely wrong about not wanting to talk about it. I responded to him by asking a question: "How else are people going to know what life is like being homeless if we don't tell them?" But he wouldn't budge. He was quite adamant about not opening up to those who had never been homeless.

Boy! Homelessness can have a profound effect on some people. And from what I observed of this guy, he was devastated by it.

***

I'm sitting in my apartment, thinking about some of the people I've met in the past year and a half. Some of them voiced strong ideas as far as how they were going to reconstruct their lives since becoming homeless.

One fellow went as far as saying that he was going to dig out a small cave in a riverbank, just big enough to sleep in. *That's a radical idea,* I thought.

Others told me how they were reevaluating their expectations, not sure if getting their own apartment, having a car, and going back to the way things used to be meant that much to them anymore. And they questioned whether going back to the way things were would really give them their independence.

It doesn't matter whether you're homeless or not, almost all people, at one time or another, have to tighten their belts to live within their means. But for those who are homeless, their standard of living takes a real blow—economic as well as psychological. In other words, it's very easy for a homeless person to give up and lose all hope.

If you let it, homelessness can cripple you way past the point of no return. The ramifications can be more harmful than we're willing to admit.

That's why homelessness needs to be put in the spotlight and given more attention. Too often good people just fall by the wayside and are never heard from again. We can't allow this to keep happening to our citizens.

In a country like ours, if you're *willing* to get your life back on track, America is still a place where it can happen. I wonder if Pink Floyd (the sixties British rock group) was thinking of America when they wrote the lyric for "Shine On You Crazy Diamond." Just a thought.

Park near the shelter where I frequently hung out.

Many days were just spent looking at the Charles River.

If I was going to make it to the five o'clock dinner at the soup kitchen, I knew I'd better get moving. On my way over to the kitchen, I met some people from the Brewster who were also on their way to the soup kitchen.

"Dave, how are you doing?" I yelled.

"Jim, haven't seen you for a while. What are you up to these days?" Dave exclaimed.

"Well, I'm doing better now than the last time I saw you," I replied. "The last I heard, you were going out west someplace."

Dave replied, "Yeah, the Dakotas. What a wasteland. Nothing going on. I almost starved to death."

"Gee, Dave, I heard there was all kinds of work out there. There's gold in them thar hills! You're telling me that's not the case?"

Dave seemed to be at a loss for words. After a short pause, he said, "I really didn't plan anything. I just packed my things and headed out west. Figured I'd make it up as I went."

"How long have you been back?"

"Only a week," he replied. "I need to find some work. I'm broke."

I told him I'd see him down at Labor Force on Monday morning.

Dave smiled, shook his head, and said, "Back to the same old grind! I guess my break hasn't come yet."

It was good to see Dave. It was obvious to me that he was going through some tough times. But knowing Dave as I did, I was sure he'd be okay.

I wasn't doing so great myself. I really needed to get my car back, but it would cost me plenty to get it back on the road again.

I kept telling myself that something would turn up, even though it seemed like nothing ever did. I was doing what I could, but it wasn't good enough. Having my own laptop would be invaluable to me. That was something I wanted to purchase as soon as I could. I was tired of having to go to the library every time I needed to use the Internet.

I was walking to the bus stop, heading back to my place. I thought I'd cut through the park that I used to frequent quite a bit. It reminded me how close to the edge of homelessness I stand.

***

Sure, I may have my own place. But it's certainly not my ideal living situation by any stretch of the imagination.

Freeing myself totally from the grip of homelessness has proven to be no easy task. Every decision I make from this point forward is critical. *I am not going back to the streets!* Having gone through that nightmare is all the reason I need to get my life in order.

However, my overall attitude toward life and how I conduct myself is changed forever. And I hate to admit that it took homelessness to make me realize this and show me a better way. The changes I'm talking about are mainly to be more responsible and to reprioritize what's important in my life. What I want to do is give back to the homeless community and not forget those I shared this awful experience with.

6

FINAL THOUGHTS

Things are starting to improve for me. I am no longer depending on homeless shelters. Another good sign is that I've already convinced myself that my homeless days are behind me. That's a bold claim, considering what I've been through. But I'm going forward and never looking back.

Finally, my car is back on the road, and I have some promising job prospects. I feel things are going to work out. Homelessness has profoundly opened my eyes and made me see and better understand what is really important.

I've always been aware of having the good fortune of being born in a free and open society. But since becoming homeless, I can appreciate it so much more.

I've experienced human kindness in its purest form. And I've watched all my flimsy, self-centered goals and dreams fall like a house of cards. My material desires were replaced by the scramble for life's necessities. My easier times turned to hard times. The difficult hurdles forced me to reevaluate my mind-set in all sorts of ways. And for me, that was tough, like having to take bad-tasting medicine.

One person can make a positive contribution that can affect many lives. And when many people unite on an issue or concern, we can move mountains. Our history tells us this. It's like an *ace up my sleeve* for humanity!

I'm not sure how our overall society looks at homelessness. I wouldn't be surprised if the majority of people are callous and indifferent to this problem. I wasn't any different before I became homeless. If I read an article on the Internet or saw a news clip on a homeless person, I wouldn't even give it a passing thought and would go on with my daily life. But now that I have experienced being homeless firsthand, I certainly want to do my part in helping those who fall victim to this terrible condition.

In conclusion, I would like to see conditions improve for the homeless, especially regarding the availability of shelters and a more reasonable and compassionate approach by staff, as discussed in this book. And when we talk about the homeless, I hope more people do not automatically condemn them but seek to better understand and help—rather than stereotype—in what is a very personal and often tragic ordeal.

ABOUT THE AUTHOR

The author was born into a military family and traveled around the world the first nine years of his life. When his father got out of the service, they settled in Baltimore. He enrolled in a trade school and began his career in the heating-and-cooling field. Throughout his life, he has been passionately involved in writing and performing music.

Printed in the United States
By Bookmasters